POCKET PORTRAITS

AGATHA CHRISTIE

The Mother of the Cozy Mystery

NANCY WEST

ADAMS MEDIA
NEW YORK AMSTERDAM/ANTWERP LONDON TORONTO
SYDNEY/MELBOURNE NEW DELHI

TO CRAIG AND SILAS, WHO LOVE HERCULE POIROT AS MUCH AS I DO.

Adams Media
An Imprint of Simon & Schuster, LLC
100 Technology Center Drive
Stoughton, MA 02072

First Adams Media hardcover edition July 2026

Interior design by Kellie Emery
Illustrations by Kim Arrington
Interior images © Adobe Stock/warmworld, Helga

Manufactured in China

10 9 8 7 6 5 4 3 2 1

Library of Congress Control Number: 2025949019

ISBN 978-1-5072-2538-7
ISBN 978-1-5072-2539-4 (ebook)

Table of Contents

Introduction

Called the "Mother of the Cozy Mystery," "Queen of Crime," and "Duchess of Death," Agatha Christie is beloved for her clever whodunits set in picturesque country villages. Among the most prolific of crime writers, she published sixty-six detective novels and fourteen collections of detective stories in her lifetime. But you may be surprised to learn there is more to Christie than her slick plot twists and quaint settings.

In *Pocket Portraits: Agatha Christie,* you'll explore the life (and mysteries) of this famed writer. Drawing on first-hand accounts in her autobiography, biographical and critical writings, and clues sleuthed from her works, this book offers a vivid inside look at everything from her idyllic childhood in Devon, England to the publication of bestsellers like *And Then There Were None.* Through one hundred biographical vignettes you'll learn about:

- The start—and end—of her first marriage
- The friendships and rivalries she enjoyed with other writers

- Her eleven-day disappearance and the police manhunt it caused
- Her secret career as a novelist beyond detective fiction and her spectacular run as a playwright
- And more

You'll also find excerpts from her best murder mysteries, including novels such as *The Murder of Roger Ackroyd* and *Crooked House* and plays like *The Mousetrap* and *Black Coffee.*

Agatha Christie's life, like her fiction, abounds in ironies and contradictions. She may have portrayed herself to the public as placid, but underneath was a highly sensitive, adventurous woman, and her seemingly conventional life contains many shocks and surprises. Born at the end of the Victorian era, she would witness, by the time of her death, two world wars, the rising use of espionage, and the end of the British Empire and start of the Cold War. She would go on archaeological expeditions to countries like Iraq and Syria, and when her first husband shockingly announced that he wanted a divorce, she would temporarily disappear without a trace.

As you read through the following vignettes, you'll tease out the themes of Christie's inner world and works: adventure, betrayal, deception, and the danger that lies beneath the surface of things. So, turn the page and let's begin, *mon amie,* as detective Hercule Poirot would say.

The Gentleman and Poor Relation

Agatha Christie's father, Frederick Alvah Miller, was born in New York City on Halloween, in 1846. His own father, Nathaniel Frary Miller, was a self-made American businessman who left Frederick a hefty fortune when he moved to England in the 1860s to remarry. Frederick, whom Agatha would later describe as a "lazy but very agreeable man," did not take over the family business. Instead, he spent his days in New York City as a gentleman about town, enjoying leisurely pursuits like Broadway shows, horse races in Saratoga Springs, and gentlemen clubs.

Born in Dublin in 1854, Agatha's mother, Clarissa ("Clara"), was Fredrick's cousin by marriage. After her father died in a horse-riding accident in 1863, nine-year-old Clara was sent to live with her English aunt, Frederick's stepmother, Margaret Miller, in London. By all accounts, Clara felt hurt and rejected. She grew quiet, losing confidence. As Agatha later wrote, Clara lacked Frederick's sureness and sociability and was "shy and miserably diffident about herself." When Clara was ten, Frederick visited London and complimented her eyes. According to Agatha, Clara never looked at another man again. Fourteen years later, in April

1878, the couple married and moved to the seaside resort of Torquay, in Devon, England.

Frederick spent his days in Torquay playing cricket, eating five-course meals, and buying home accessories. A compulsive shopper, Christie biographer Lucy Worsley notes, he had to extend the family house twice to make room for his purchases. Clara, a natural at domestic matters despite her shyness, made a comfortable home and managed the household. Wildly imaginative according to Agatha, Clara also wrote poetry and fiction in her spare time. She would become Agatha's first literary role model.

Agatha would remember Frederick and Clara as "two people who loved each other dearly" and gave her "a very happy childhood," though troubles lurked in the Miller home . . .

THE MORE YOU KNOW

Frederick grew up during New York City's "Gilded Age." Coined by Mark Twain in 1873, this term refers to the huge economic growth in America, especially New York City, between 1865 and 1900 and the concentration of wealth among those like John D. Rockefeller and Andrew Carnegie. The Gilded Age was also a time of spectacular material excess. (You can learn more about this period by reading Twain's novel, *The Gilded Age: A Tale of Today* (1873), or the fiction of Edith Wharton, or by watching Julian Fellowes's TV series *The Gilded Age*.)

Bloody Lady Agatha

Agatha was a surprise addition to the Miller family, an "afterthought," as she would describe herself. Born on September 15, 1890, she was a child of the Victorian fin de siècle (or "end of the century"). Her siblings, Margaret ("Madge"), born in 1879, and Louis ("Monty"), born in 1880, were eleven and ten, respectively.

Photographed with large hazel eyes and massive golden hair, Agatha was a happy child. Her autobiography, written between 1950 and 1965, recounts how much she relished the pleasures of home: piano lessons; swims in the cove; and afternoon teas of cakes and cream. Yet beneath the sunshine, a dark imagination lurked. At age five, she began having nightmares of someone she called the "Gunman," a uniformed Frenchman who carried a musket. Later in her youth, the Gunman would appear in her dreams to be a friend or family member, then suddenly turn into a stranger. "The dream would be quite ordinary. . . . Then suddenly a horrid feeling of uneasiness would come. . . . Sometimes . . . I would look across at a friend, or a member of the family, and I would suddenly realise that it was not Dorothy . . . or whoever it might be. The pale blue eyes in the familiar face met mine—under the familiar appearance. *It was really the Gunman*."

Her imagination developed quickly, enriched by her mother, Clara, and older sister, Madge. Clara invented bedtime stories for Agatha, almost never telling the same story twice. When home from school, Madge would take her little sister to the theater and regale Agatha with humorous accounts of her friends and activities. Madge also loved performing in and inventing plays, and Agatha would act out roles with her.

At age ten, Agatha wrote her first poem, "The Cowslip." Around the same time, she invented a story about the noble Lady Madge and bloody Lady Agatha, a Gothic melodrama that involved the inheritance of a castle. It was very short, Agatha would explain, because "both writing and spelling were a pain to me." When Clara primly suggested she shouldn't use the word "bloody," Agatha protested, "But she *was* bloody. She killed a lot of people." And so emerged Agatha's first portrait of a serial killer.

LITERARY CONNECTIONS

Agatha was born just a year before the first Sherlock Holmes story, "A Scandal in Bohemia," appeared in *The Strand* magazine. But when it comes to late-nineteenth-century detective fiction, Sir Arthur Conan Doyle wasn't the only name in town. Plenty of women were writing detective stories too. One was Anna Katharine Green, whose 1878 novel, *The Leavenworth Case,* launched a detective series featuring Ebenezer Gryce. In the latter novel, Gryce gets help from society spinster Amelia Butterworth.

Educating Agatha

Progressive for her Victorian upbringing, Clara sent both Monty *and* Madge off to boarding school. But when Madge came home more studious than Frederick preferred—"We can't have Madge turned into a bluestocking," he reportedly said—Clara decided that her younger daughter would be educated at home. (In the eighteenth and nineteenth centuries, an intellectually minded woman was called a "bluestocking.") What's more, Agatha wouldn't be taught to read until she was eight, as Clara believed this delay was better for the development of the eyes and brain.

Things didn't go according to Clara's plan. On walks, Agatha would ask her nurse ("Nursie," as Agatha called her) what the words written over shops and on billboards were. At home, she'd study the pages of the books she liked best—until one day, when Agatha was four, Nursie said to Clara, "I'm afraid, Ma'am, Miss Agatha *can* read."

Clara got her way on the homeschooling front, however. Frederick started teaching his daughter to write at age five. He also taught Agatha mathematics each morning, while Clara schooled her in history, or rather those parts of history Clara found interesting. Madge, when home from school, supplemented Frederick's lessons in writing. She tried to teach her younger sister French as well, but Agatha found her such a bad teacher, she hid the manual. Monty and Frederick helped Agatha with mandolin and piano lessons.

Much of Agatha's education also happened alone in a book-lined "schoolroom" at the top of the Miller house. A solitary and curious girl, as biographers would describe her, Agatha devoured *Jane Eyre, Robinson Crusoe, Little Women,* and an assortment of children's fiction popular in the late nineteenth century.

It was a ragtag education in a house overflowing with books, atlases, and encyclopedias. And as Christie biographer Laura Thompson suggests, it was "probably the making of" Agatha. In interviews, the author would claim she had little education growing up. Such statements were part of an effort to fashion herself as an ordinary woman. Her autobiography, however, reveals that she received a first-rate education at home and during the time she spent in Paris, both at age seven and again as a teenager.

LITERARY CONNECTIONS

The 1890s were part of the "Golden Era of Children's Literature" (spanning the mid-1860s to the mid-1920s). This era saw a boom in the number and quality of children's books as well as a shift from moralizing, didactic tales to more imaginative ones. Among the era's best-loved books are *The Adventures of Pinocchio* (1883), *The Jungle Books* (1894, 1895), and *The Wonderful Wizard of Oz* (1900).

Nursie and Co.

Situated on a hill above Torquay, the Miller home of Ashfield was a Victorian villa set in a 2-acre garden with a greenhouse, orchid house, and many varieties of trees. Frederick and Clara bought it in 1881. They had planned to move to New York City, but when Clara saw the house, she knew she had to have it. Agatha would recall Ashfield as the single most important place of her life. When it was torn down in the early 1960s, she "cried like a child," according to Laura Thompson. For the author, it provided a unique combination of security, freedom, and order during her childhood.

While her parents gave Agatha a sense of safety and the freedom to read and explore as she pleased, Ashfield's servants kept order in the house and in her upbringing. Jane Rowe, the cook, single-handedly produced five-course meals daily (it was Rowe who instilled in Agatha a lifelong passion for Devonshire cream); Susan Lewis, or Nursie, was "the rock of stability" in Agatha's life, making sure that Agatha was dressed, fed, entertained, and exercised. Jane Ratcliffe and Charlotte Froud, along with a succession of parlormaids, cleaned and tidied the house, and William Callicott tended Ashfield's gardens.

The servants ensured order, but it was Clara's spirit—creative, impulsive, rule breaking—that presided over Ashfield.

Clara was seen as timid and hesitant in public, but at home, she was described as a force, making most of the domestic decisions. She organized elaborate dinner parties whose guests included Henry James and Rudyard Kipling, and she managed the Ashfield staff with what scholar Rachel Trethewey describes as "a natural authority." Dressed in colorful floral tunics or flowing indoor coats of black marocain (just like Frederica Rice in Christie's *Peril at End House*), she would walk around the house reciting lines from Alfred, Lord Tennyson.

Clara and the four female servants—along with Agatha, Madge, and their grandmothers, Margaret Miller ("Auntie-Grannie") and Polly Boehmer ("Grannie B")—formed a matriarchal household. It was the women at Ashfield who ran things, and Christie scholars believe that this strong feminine influence shaped Agatha and inspired the prominence she gives to women, and women's lives, in her books. (More on that later.)

LITERARY CONNECTIONS

On New Year's Eve in 1892, William Callicott hanged himself with a rope in a disused stable at Ashfield. His body was discovered by Frederick Miller, who had been out that night touring the gardens. Callicott left no note of explanation. Only two years old at the time of the incident, Agatha would use Callicott's suicide for a similar scene in her semi-autobiographical novel, *Unfinished Portrait.*

The English Riviera

Coined in the nineteenth century to announce its rivalry with France's popular seaside area, the "English Riviera" refers to the 22-mile stretch of coves, fishing villages, and seaside resorts along South Devon's coast. It is here that Agatha Christie grew up at Ashfield.

On the Devon coast, Agatha became a strong and athletic swimmer. As a young child, she would remain in the sea much longer than other children. Sometimes she swam alone, supervised by Auntie-Grannie, and often with Madge and Monty when they were home from school. As a young Edwardian woman, Agatha used a "bathing machine" when she went swimming. Bathing machines were roofed and walled carts that carried men and women out to the ocean while they changed into their "bathing costumes," thereby ensuring privacy and respectability. Agatha described her own costume as an "unaesthetic garment" made of "numerous skirts, flounces, and frills, reaching well down below" the knees.

Distinguished by its cliffs and isolated spots, the Devon coast would serve as the setting for many Christie murders. For example, Burgh Island, accessible at high tide only by an aquatic motor vehicle called a "sea tractor," is thought to have inspired Christie's depiction of the remote Soldier Island in

And Then There Were None (1939). Spoiler alert: In *Evil Under the Sun* (1941), Christine Redfern murders actress Arlena Marshall on the isolated Pixy Cove, then swims back to her hotel in record time to establish an alibi. In *Towards Zero* (1944), tennis pro Nevile Strange swims across ocean waters and scales a cliff to murder his aunt, Lady Tressilian. And in *Peril at End House* (1932), Poirot and Captain Arthur Hastings vacation in Devon, where they meet a serial murderer.

Visting the English Riviera today, you can find Agatha Christie commemorations everywhere. In Torquay, you can walk the Agatha Christie Mile, featuring the author's favorite bathing cove; the Torre Abbey Gardens, specializing in poisonous plants; and Greenway, the Georgian-style house on 33 acres that Christie bought in 1938 and used as a family retreat. You can also see a life-sized statue of Christie. Unveiled in the spring of 2025, it depicts Agatha sitting on a bench with her beloved dog, Peter.

LITERARY CONNECTIONS

Starting in the 1920s, the English Riviera developed into a popular vacation spot as the rage for swimming and sunbathing took hold of England, America, and continental Europe. The narrator of Christie's *Evil Under the Sun* comments on this phenomenon in the novel's opening chapter, explaining, "In 1922 when the great cult of the Seaside for Holidays was finally established and the coast of Devon and Cornwall was no longer thought too hot in the summer . . ."

From And Then There Were None, Chapter 4

"Yes," he said. "It's pleasant. It's a good place, I think, to wait."

"To wait?" said Vera sharply. "What are you waiting for?"

He said gently:

"The end. But I think you know that, don't you? It's true, isn't it? We're all waiting for the end."

She said unsteadily:

"What do you mean?"

General Macarthur said gravely:

"None of us are going to leave the island. "That's the plan."

Clever Madge

"Witty, very entertaining, quick of repartee, and successful in everything she attempted," according to Agatha, Margaret "Madge" Frary Miller was Agatha's older sister and the eldest child of Frederick and Clara. Born on January 9, 1879, in Torquay, Madge was a laughing, boisterous girl who loved pranks and jokes; she was thought by everyone in the Christie family to have inherited her father's gaiety and humor. Like Agatha, she shared Clara's creative genius and writerly interests. And while Agatha was the "slow" one in the family, as she describes herself, Madge thought, spoke, and moved like wildfire.

Eleven years separated Madge and Agatha. In fact, Madge was already at the Miss Lawrences' boarding school in Brighton when Agatha was born. But the two sisters were close, especially in their youth, and little Agatha was, by all accounts, awed by her talented sister. Possessed of an innate gift for acting, Madge loved to invent dramas in which she played colorful characters; as Agatha tells it, one of Madge's favorite roles as a teenager was the evil "Elder Sister" who suffered from madness and lived in a cave. This Elder Sister was older than Madge but, according to Agatha, "indistinguishable in appearance" except for her voice—a "frightening voice," as Agatha would describe it, "soft" and "oily." The Elder Sister would say, "You know who I am, don't you, dear? I'm your sister Madge. You don't think I'm anyone else, do you? You wouldn't think *that*?" Madge was also the one who introduced Agatha to Sherlock Holmes by reading stories like "The Adventure of the Blue Carbuncle" and "The Five Orange Pips" aloud to her.

An ambitious and gifted student, Madge excelled in her coursework at the Miss Lawrences' School. At fourteen or fifteen, she went to finishing school in Paris, returning in "a gay little straw hat and a white veil with black spots on it;" to Agatha, she appeared as "an entirely new person." In January 1896, when she was seventeen and Agatha five, Madge made a spectacular debut into society at the Waldorf Hotel in New York City, accompanied by her father, Frederick, and greeted by none other than well-known socialite Caroline Astor.

LITERARY CONNECTIONS

In her autobiography, Agatha mentions that Madge published several stories in *Vanity Fair* before Madge got married. She didn't write professionally again until 1924 when, at age forty-five, she wrote a play called *The Claimant*, which caught the eye of a high-profile producer. *The Claimant* ran for several weeks in the West End of London with moderate success.

"He'll Never Get Anywhere"

"A source of trouble and worry" to the Millers is how Agatha would describe her brother, Louis Montant ("Monty") Miller. The only son of Frederick and Clara, Monty was born on June 23, 1880, in New Jersey, where his parents were briefly visiting relatives.

By all accounts, Monty was a lively and naughty child. When walking down a street with Madge, for example, six-year-old Monty would push her into a sweetshop, order "three pennyworth" of candy, and then dare her not to pay. He teased Agatha by calling her a "scrawny chicken," which made her "burst into tears," as she recalled. Good with his hands, Monty kept a workshop at Ashfield as a teenager and owned a small dinghy. One day he took Agatha out on the boat. The sea was choppy, and she threw up three times, returning to Ashfield green in the face. According to Agatha, he landed her in "high disgust," remarking that "women were all the same."

But Monty was known to have a soft side too. As a child, he owned an old dog named Scotty, and when he was home from school, the two of them were inseparable. According to Agatha, Monty would lie flat on the floor and put his face up to the dog's while hugging him tenderly. While other family members complained of Scotty's smell, Monty would say, "Roses! That's what he smells of—roses."

At his boarding school, Harrow, which he entered around the age of ten, Monty couldn't pass his exams. However, he had a gift for talking his superiors into anything (apparently, he was the only Harrow student to keep white mice). "He'll never get anywhere," said the owner of a shipbuilding yard where Monty later tried to find work. Apparently, the problem was math. "You see, he can't do mathematics," the owner told Frederick. "You show him anything practical and it's all right; he's a good practical workman. But that's all he'll ever be in the engineering line."

Nevertheless, Monty possessed certain talents that entranced Agatha as a child. He could play several instruments by ear and had a rich, bass voice. Like his father, Monty knew how to attract people: His manners in society were exquisite, his charm boundless. When Madge, for example, raged at him for tricking her at the candy shop, Monty would "merely smile at her serenely and offer her one of the sweets," according to Agatha.

The More You Know

Harrow, the boarding school Monty attended, dates back to 1572. It boasts among its graduates Lord Byron, Winston Churchill, and Benedict Cumberbatch. The school was founded to provide free education to thirty (later forty) poor boys of the parish. "Foreigners," or boys outside the parish, were admitted on the payment of fees. It was the need for foreigners to find accommodation that led to the concept of a "boarding" school.

The Album of Confessions

As Agatha and her siblings were growing and maturing, a long-honored Miller tradition was keeping track of it all. Bound in a leather case, the "Album of Confessions" contained an extensive list of questions to which members of the family would write down their answers after each passing year. And they weren't the only family with such an album. These albums were a highly popular pastime in nineteenth-century England and America. A prototype of the "personality quiz," the album posed questions designed to get at a person's character by revealing their values, tastes, interests, and ambitions.

In her autobiography, Agatha refers to the Millers' Album of Confessions, as do Christie biographies. Here are some of the questions and answers from the Millers' album:

Q: If not yourself, who would you be?
A: "A better man" (Monty Miller); "A fairy" (Agatha, age four)

Q: What is your pet aversion?
A: "Bedtime, when you're awake" (Agatha, age seven); "Getting up in the morning" (Frederick)

Q: What is your present state of mind?
A: "Anxious" (Clara)

Q: What is your idea of happiness?
A: "To make the best of everything" (Agatha, age thirteen)

Q: What is your favorite food?
A: "Beefsteak, Chops, Apple Fritters, Peaches, Apples. All kinds of nuts. More peaches. More nuts. Irish stew. Roly Poly Pudding. Bitter Beer" (Frederick)

Q: What is your favorite pastime?
A: "Doing nothing" (Frederick)

Q: What is your chief characteristic?
A: "Living in the present" (Agatha, age thirteen); "Getting on with it" (Madge, age sixteen)

Q: What is your idea of misery?
A: "For someone I love to go away from me" (Agatha, age seven); "Borrowing money" (Monty)

Q: What is your favorite drink?
A: "Cherry brandy" (Grannie-B)

Q: What is your present state of mind?
A: "Extremely comfortable, thank you" (Frederick)

Q: If not yourself, who would you be?
A: "Nobody" (Frederick; Agatha, age thirteen)

Agatha would continue the album tradition throughout her life (though it's unknown whether she used the original Miller album or started her own). In 1954, the album described her "present state" as "deeply happy." Her last entry, written when she was in her seventies, would be to the question "If not yourself, who would you be?" Her answer: "An opera singer."

LITERARY CONNECTIONS

Hercule Poirot alludes to the Album of Confessions in his exchange with Rosamund Darnley in *Evil Under the Sun*: "When I was young (and that, Mademoiselle, is indeed a long time ago), there was a game entitled 'If not yourself who would you be?' One wrote the answer in young ladies' albums. They had gold edges and were bound in blue leather. The answer? Mademoiselle, is not really very easy to find."

The Millers, Ruined

Sometime in the late 1890s, when Agatha was eight or nine, she declared to her tutor that the Miller family was financially "ruined." As she would later recount, Clara reprimanded her: "Really, Agatha . . . We are *not* ruined. We are just badly off for the time being and will have to economise." But the truth is, Agatha was closer to being right than Clara indicated.

Agatha's American grandfather, Nathaniel Frary Miller, had made the family fortune by working his way up from clerk to partner in the dry goods company H.B. Claflin & Company. He supplemented that fortune with investments in New York City properties. Nathaniel, by all accounts, had a gift for making money. But Agatha's father had a gift for spending it. He understood very little of his father's business, having never worked there. Instead, he received company dividends while never questioning the decisions of Claflin's managers or trustees. As Agatha would explain in her autobiography, "He had been a rich man's son and had taken it for granted that an assured income would always come in." By 1895, however, the family's holdings were suddenly yielding diminishing returns.

It was a shock for the Millers, who believed they were comfortably off for life. (Several Christie biographers speculate that Frederick may have been cheated by some of the family fund's trustees.) As finances dwindled, Frederick considered looking for a job, though he wasn't qualified for anything. And Monty could only be trusted to squander whatever money remained. Then there was Madge's debutante season to attend to, which involved hosting events that would introduce Madge, now seventeen, to an array of wealthy potential male suitors. Rather than minimize expenses, Frederick took his daughter on a four-month trip to New York City to launch her coming out. They sailed home with thirteen trunks of luggage.

Frederick's one practical step toward improving finances was to rent out Ashfield, an expensive house to run, and have the family—he, Clara, and seven-year-old Agatha—live abroad in France for a year sometime between 1896 and 1897. The action, common among English upper-class people who felt the need to economize, saved the family some money but nowhere near enough. Agatha, who'd never thought about money before, could now see that her parents were troubled—and that all their worry was making her father ill.

LITERARY CONNECTIONS

In Christie's novels, you can find many financiers, bankers, and investors who commit dastardly acts. The most famous of Agatha's high-profile crooks lurks in *Death on the Nile* (1937), which features Andrew Pennington as an embezzler who tries to steal the fortune of a young heiress named Linnet Ridgeway. You can also see these villainous characters in such early stories as "The Lost Mine" (1923) and "The Disappearance of Mr. Davenheim" (1924).

From Death on the Nile, Chapter 10

"What's the big idea, then?"

Pennington smoothed out the letter on the table.

"Linnet's going to Egypt for her honeymoon. Expects to be there for a month or more . . ."

"Egypt-eh?"

Rockford considered. Then he looked up and met the other's glance.

"Egypt," he said; "*that's* your idea!"

"Yes, a chance meeting. Over on a trip. Linnet and her husband—honeymoon atmosphere. It might be done."

Rockford said doubtfully:

"She's sharp, Linnet is . . . but—"

Pennington said softly: "I think there might be ways of—managing it."

Again their eyes met. Rockford nodded.

"Alright big boy."

Pennington looked at the clock.

"We'll have to hustle—whichever of us is going."

"You go," said Rockford promptly. "You always made a hit with Linnet. 'Uncle Andrew.' That's the ticket!"

Pennington's face had hardened.

A List of Heart Attacks

Frederick first felt poorly while the family was living in France during Ashfield's rental. Suffering attacks of pain and breathlessness in the night, he consulted a few doctors in Paris, one of whom diagnosed kidney disease. When the family returned from France to Ashfield, Frederick's doctor in Torquay disagreed with the diagnosis but couldn't offer an alternative one. A battery of tests was run, all of them inconclusive.

It was clear that Frederick was very ill. Between April 1899 and September 1901, he recorded a list of forty-five "heart attacks" he suffered (most likely, these attacks were angina, a chest pain or discomfort that occurs when the heart doesn't receive enough oxygen-rich blood). Frederick continued seeking treatments, traveling to one specialist who, as he wrote Clara, advised "plenty of fresh air, distilled water, milk after meals and later perhaps cod liver oil or Extract of Malt."

For a while, he continued living life as he always had—spending time at his yacht club, watching croquet, and enjoying big meals. But this didn't last. In late October 1901, he saw a specialist in Ealing, London, while visiting Auntie-Grannie. Less than a month later, while in Ealing again, he caught a cold, which quickly turned into double pneumonia. Clara, Agatha, and Madge raced to Ealing to be with him (Monty, who was fighting in the Second Boer War at the time, didn't respond to Clara's telegram or later attend the funeral). Then, on November 26, 1901, at age fifty-five, Frederick Miller died.

Years later, Agatha found the last letter he wrote to Clara. "You have made all the difference in my life," it said. His death devastated his wife. Agatha tried to console Clara, telling her that "Father is at peace now. . . . You wouldn't want him back, would you?" Reflecting on her statement many years later, she described it as the kind of sentiment that churchgoing children like her had "been *told* is right, and what they *know* is right, but which they feel may . . . be *wrong*." According to Agatha, Clara "reared up in bed with a violent gesture" and answered, "Yes, I would. I would do anything in the world to have him back. . . ." Clara suddenly seemed entirely different from the mother Agatha knew. As Lucy Worsley writes, "Her mother had become a stranger. It was as if the Gun Man had dared to penetrate even the familiar surroundings of Clara's own bedroom."

THE MORE YOU KNOW

Modern cardiology emerged as a field of medicine during the period shortly before Frederick suffered his heart trouble. Three inventions led to this emergence: the X-ray as a diagnostic tool in 1895; the sphygmomanometer, a device used to measure blood pressure, in 1881; and the electrocardiograph in 1902.

Postmortem

"It was the end of my childhood," Agatha later wrote of her father's death. "I wandered about the house in a queer state of turmoil.... The blinds of the house were pulled down, the lamps were lit. . . . In her big chair, Grannie sat writing endless letters.... From time to time she shook her head sadly."

Of all the Miller family, however, Clara was said to have suffered the worst, experiencing panic attacks and developing heart ailments. Agatha later described how she would wake up at night, panicked Clara might die. She'd then listen outside Clara's door to make sure she was still breathing. She even set up a camp bed in her mother's dressing room to ensure that if Clara became ill, she'd be there.

Within a year or so, Clara recovered, at least partly, and started pouring her energy into raising Agatha. She took her to the Torquay theater and read Charles Dickens and William Makepeace Thackeray aloud to her in the evenings. Years later, when seventeen-year-old Agatha was sick in bed, Clara encouraged her to write a story. When Agatha expressed doubt she could do it, Clara replied, "Of course you can, darling. You just begin *now*." Clara brought her an exercise book, and Agatha began writing. The result was a six-thousand-word, semi-autobiographical story, "The House of Beauty," eventually published as "The House of Dreams" in January 1926.

In poor health, Clara rarely went out, but, as scholar Rachel Trethewey explains, she was very mindful of her daughter's need for socializing. Clara encouraged Agatha to go to parties and enrolled her at Miss Guyer's Girls' School in 1902. When Agatha was fifteen, Clara sent her to a sequence of Parisian finishing schools—an opportunity she herself didn't have as a child.

How did Clara afford all this now that the family fortune was gone? The Millers were only "ruined" in the sense that they couldn't live as extravagantly as before. Clara received 300 pounds per year from Frederick's estate after he died, while Agatha got 100 pounds a year from a trust established by Frederick's father, Nathaniel. (The average income in Britain at this time was 42 pounds per year.) Mother and daughter weren't poor, but they had to adjust to a less wealthy way of life. This ability to adapt was something Agatha later claimed as one of her strongest qualities.

LITERARY CONNECTIONS

In 1934, Agatha Christie published *Unfinished Portrait,* which Max Mallowan, Christie's second husband, identified as the "most autobiographical of all her novels." A central aspect of the book is the protagonist's close relationship with her mother. In it, Agatha describes how the mother would smile at her daughter and squeeze her hand, "as though they two had a secret shared." Another line reads, "Her mother—oh, there was no one like her mother in the whole world!"

An "Excellent Chest and Splendid Expansion"

During the two winters and one summer she spent at Parisian finishing schools, Agatha studied piano and voice. Her dream at this age was to become a musician. At Mademoiselle Tschimi's, the first finishing school she went to in Paris (Madge had also gone there), she learned how to read music while performing a *quatre mains* with her teacher, Madame Legrand. According to Agatha, Legrand would become so absorbed in her own vigorous playing that she wouldn't even notice when Agatha had lost her place in the piece. Several times, she almost pushed Agatha off the piano bench.

From Mademoiselle T's, Agatha went for a few months to Les Marroniers, which Clara reportedly found unsatisfactory because they spoke too much English there, then to Miss Dryden's. At Miss Dryden's, she took piano lessons with an Austrian named Charles Fürster, whom she would describe as a "good but frightening teacher." Under Fürster, Agatha practiced Chopin and Tchaikovsky seven hours a day. A "wild hope," as she would call it, was starting to grow: to become a concert pianist.

It was also at Miss Dryden's that Agatha took singing lessons from a teacher named Monsieur Boué. He lived in an apartment five flights up with no elevator, and Agatha recalled that by the time she got to his apartment, she'd always be out of breath. Boué reproached her, saying that someone her age "should spring upstairs, without panting." Then, he'd measure her diaphragm as she did breathing exercises. "You have a good chest," he'd tell her, "an excellent chest. You have splendid expansion, and what is more . . . you will never have the consumption."

Before she left Paris at age seventeen, she asked Fürster if he thought she could become a concert pianist. He told her that she didn't have "the temperament to play in public." Agatha later described this as the end of her "wild hope," writing that "if the thing you want beyond anything cannot be, it is much better to recognize it and go forward."

Returning home to Ashfield sometime in 1906 or 1907, Agatha went forward with a new "wild hope" to become a writer.

THE MORE YOU KNOW

Agatha also had hopes of becoming an opera singer. A family friend connected with the Metropolitan Opera House of New York City came to hear her sing at Ashfield shortly after she returned home from Paris for good. After taking the seventeen-year-old Agatha through arias (solo opera songs) and exercises, he said, "You will make a good concert singer and should be able to do well and make a name at that. Your voice is *not* strong enough for opera and never will be."

Introducing Miss Miller

When Agatha turned seventeen in 1907, Clara arranged a debutante season for her, as she and Frederick had done with Madge. However, with Frederick gone and money limited, Clara couldn't show off her younger daughter quite as lavishly. Instead, in January 1908, mother and daughter set sail for Cairo, Egypt, which had its own expatriate social season. Here, Agatha's debut could be done more affordably. During this three-month trip to Egypt, Agatha attended five dances a week and got to know "at least twenty or thirty young men reasonably well." At these events, she attracted many eligible suitors in her upper-middle-class circle and was proposed to nine times—and engaged twice—before a young man named Archie Christie came along. (But more on that later.)

Amid the courtships, Agatha began her first novel, *Snow upon the Desert*, a romantic novel set in Cairo. Like much of her later work, it focuses on well-heeled characters thrown together in an exotic location, employs a light touch when it comes to description and dialogue, and features a male protagonist with Byronic sex appeal.

When she came home from Egypt in the spring of 1908, Christie sent *Snow upon the Desert* to Eden Phillpotts, a celebrated local writer. He read her manuscript and wrote back with detailed feedback. "You have a great feeling for dialogue," he said (calling out what would become one of Agatha Christie's most celebrated qualities as a writer). He also advised her to "cut all moralisations out of your novels . . . . Try and leave your characters *alone*, so that *they* can speak for *themselves*." It was advice she took seriously; years later, she would have a reputation among readers as a ruthless and detached writer, willing to murder off likable characters. Agatha sent *Snow upon the Desert* to several publishers. But it came back each time, rejected. The problem wasn't characterization or dialogue, according to Lucy Worsley; "It was the ridiculous plot," featuring a heroine who loses her hearing.

Snow upon the Desert never did get published. It remains in the Christie Archive Trust in Torquay, available to scholars but largely unknown to the reading public.

LITERARY CONNECTIONS

Born in 1862, Eden Phillpotts was a playwright, poet, and novelist who lived in Devon. He is perhaps best known for his Dartmoor cycle of novels, which depict the lives of people living on the moors. Agatha dedicated her 1932 novel, *Peril at End House*, to him.

From Snow upon the Desert (Unpublished Manuscript, Opening to Chapter 1)

"Rosamund," said Lady Charminster, "is an amazing girl!" Then fearing that perhaps she had not done herself justice, she added, with a flash of inspiration: "She can neither be ignored nor explained!"

This was distinctly good. Lady Charminster felt that she had never done better. It was terse, it was apt, it was one of those concise sayings that have a certain backing of truth to their epigrammatic force . . .

Of course, anywhere but in Cairo, Lady Charminster reflected, she would not have been sitting beside Connie Ansell, but Egypt, in its social sense, was distinctly limited.

Nine Proposals

In her autobiography, Agatha hints that she was proposed to nine times during her debutante season. The first proposal came from a man named Captain Hibberd, who first asked for Clara's blessing. Clara refused him, but didn't tell Agatha about the proposal until they were sailing back from Cairo. Agatha recalled being indignant, "I really do think, Mother, that you might let me have my own proposals."

Another proposal came from Colonel Bolton Fletcher, whom Agatha met while riding sidesaddle on a horse. Fletcher was thirty-five to Agatha's twenty, and very rich. He pursued her with love letters and extravagant presents, and at their third meeting, he proposed. Agatha asked him to wait six months for her answer before proposing again. When he sent a telegram six months later requesting a firm reply, she said no. Why she said no remains a mystery.

Then came a proposal from Royal Navy man Wilfred Pirie, whom Agatha's grandmother Grannie B disliked, reportedly because he neither smoked nor drank and spent too much time reading theosophy. Agatha later described him as polite but boring, confessing that his kisses "left her cold." Nevertheless, Agatha said yes. Although the reason isn't known for sure, Christie scholar Laura Thompson speculates that a marriage to Pirie presented both safety and independence. The Millers and the Piries were close friends—and with Wilfred gone much of the time to the Navy, Agatha could continue living at Ashfield. But on the day Pirie set sail for South America on a treasure-hunting expedition, Agatha called the engagement off. A few months later, Pirie married someone else.

Reggie Lucy was the last man to propose to Agatha before Archie Christie entered the picture. A major in The Gunners (a British regiment of artillery soldiers who operate and fire large guns), Lucy reportedly made Agatha feel comfortable and understood. He proposed to her during a leave from his regiment, sometime in the summer of 1912. According to Agatha, the proposal went like this: "You've got a lot of scalps, haven't you, Agatha? Well, you can put mine with them any time you like."

Lucy knew he wouldn't be returning to Devon for two years (his regiment was stationed overseas). He told Agatha to consider herself free while he was away. The gesture turned out to be Lucy's mistake.

THE MORE YOU KNOW

In *Making Marriage Modern* (2009), historian Christina Simmons charts the emergence in the early 1900s of a cultural ideal called the "companionate marriage." Privileging romantic love over convenience or economics, this ideal championed sexual and emotional intimacy between men and women. The term also embraced the right to divorce and use birth control.

Husband #1

While Reggie Lucy was away, Agatha fell in love with Archibald ("Archie") Christie. They met at a ball in Devon on October 12, 1912, where he asked her for three dances. After two, he asked for three more. According to Agatha, her dance card was full, but he told her to scratch the other names off the list. She later noted that "he had . . . an air of being able to get his own way always."

Tall and lean with thick, wavy hair, Archie was a former second lieutenant in the Royal Field Artillery. He had recently joined the Royal Flying Corps when the two met. Archie was twenty-three, Agatha twenty-two. At the time, he had no money, and although he wanted to forge a career in aviation, he didn't have any prospects. Regardless, Archie pursued Agatha, determined to make her his wife.

Sure enough, Archie proposed on the night of January 2, less than three months after the couple met. That evening, he had taken Agatha to a concert at the Pavilion in Torquay and, once they got back to Ashfield, told her, "You've got to marry me, you've *got* to marry me." He was due to leave in two days to join the Royal Flying Corps. Clara opposed the match, citing his lack of money and, according to Agatha, finding him inconsiderate and even "ruthless." But Agatha was determined to marry him. It would take almost two years—and some arguments, once over a Christmas present that she called an "absurd extravagance." Then, on August 4, 1914, England joined World War I and Archie went to France. During his leaves, he'd alternate between telling Agatha they couldn't marry and declaiming that he couldn't live without her.

Finally, during a holiday visit to his mother in Bristol, on December 23, 1914, Archie declared that they must be wed the next day. And so, on Christmas Eve, the couple were married in Archie's parish church. Twenty-four-year-old Agatha wore an everyday outfit (most likely a skirt and sweater or a wool suit), the music was courtesy of an organist who happened to be practicing, and the only witness was a friend who happened to be passing the church just as the couple showed up. Several days later, Archie returned to the war. Monty Miller went to war too, only to suffer a wound that would plague him for the rest of his life. (More on this later.)

THE MORE YOU KNOW

Popular in the nineteenth and early-twentieth centuries, dance cards were passport-sized booklets in which a woman recorded the names of the men with whom she intended to dance at a ball. According to social historians, dance cards gave women a rare opportunity to express their preference in men; they could single out those whose company they wanted and turn down others simply by saying, "My dance card is full."

Lessons in Poison

At the start of World War I in 1914, Agatha began serving as part of the Voluntary Aid Dispatch (VAD) in Torquay. "It was hard, messy, evil-smelling, tiring work," notes Christie biographer Janet Morgan. Agatha cleaned bedpans, removed lice, and stopped hemorrhages. She also witnessed amputations and watched soldiers die.

In July 1915, Agatha began working at the hospital's new dispensary, where medicines were prepared and provided. Having an aptitude for math, Agatha would recall being drawn to the calculations and classifications involved in dispensing medications. She aced the exam that qualified her to dispense medicine to chemists and medical officers, then earned her First Aid and Home Nurse certifications.

Agatha soon became fascinated by how a drug could become poisonous in the wrong dose. She observed how frequently mistakes were made, recounting an incident where she witnessed an experienced chemist make a potentially fatal mistake by misplacing a decimal point in a prescription. Rather than confront him or hand out the wrong dosage, she pretended to drop the mixture on the floor.

By all accounts, it was moments like these that led Agatha to first consider writing a detective story. The use of poison in mysteries wasn't new (in fact, poisoning was a "defining feature" of Golden Age detective fiction, according to chemist-turned-writer Kathryn Harkup), and Christie would use poison frequently in her works. More than half of her murderers choose poison as their weapon. Over the years, Christie collected a small library of toxicology books and consulted experts to expand her knowledge of poisons and fact-check the descriptions in her writing. Agatha's first use of poison as a plot device would occur in her debut novel, *The Mysterious Affair at Styles*, written while she was working in the hospital dispensary. (More on this later.)

The More You Know

According to Kathryn Harkup in her book, *A is for Arsenic: The Poisons of Agatha Christie*, Christie's poisons fall into three categories: home (pesticides and cleaning products: *Murder Is Easy*, 1939, and *Mrs. McGinty's Dead*, 1952); garden (plants and fungi: *Appointment with Death*, 1938, and *Five Little Pigs*, 1942); and medicinal (prescriptions, tonics, and remedies: *Sad Cypress*, 1940, and *One, Two, Buckle My Shoe*, 1940).

From A Pocket Full of Rye, Chapter 2

"I understand the symptoms came on immediately he had drunk the tea?"

"That's what they say."

"Well, there are very few poisons that act as quickly as that, apart from the cyanides, of course—and possibly pure nicotine—"

"And it definitely was cyanide or nicotine?"

"My dear fellow. He'd have been dead before the ambulance arrived. Oh no, there's no question of anything of that kind. I *did* suspect strychnine, but the convulsions were not at all typical. Still unofficial, of course, but I'll stake my reputation it's taxine."

"How long would that take to work?"

"Depends. An hour. Two hours, three hours. Deceased looked like a heavy eater. If he had a big breakfast, that would slow things up."

On a Bet

Agatha Christie first recounted how she became a detective writer in her autobiography. She had grown up reading crime novels like Dickens's *Bleak House,* William Wilkie Collins's *The Moonstone,* the Sherlock Holmes stories, and the detective works of Gaston Leroux. It was while discussing Leroux with Madge that Agatha said she'd like to try writing her own detective story. Madge replied that she didn't think she could do it, which set Agatha off writing.

The result was *The Mysterious Affair at Styles,* which Christie began writing in 1916 while working at the hospital dispensary. In this novel, the victim is killed by strychnine, a highly toxic, odorless poison. *Styles* also features Cynthia Murdoch, a young woman who, like Agatha, works at a hospital dispensary. It's Cynthia's knowledge of poisons that helps solve the case. In 1916, the Sherlock Holmes stories were still wildly popular, and Christie blended elements of the Holmes canon (a likable assistant of average intelligence; a final, explanatory scene) into her work. Yet even in *Styles,* one can see her own distinctive features at play, including a country house setting and a limited number of suspects.

In fact, *Styles* was a template for the Christie books to come. In *Styles,* she set up her golden principle regarding plot:

"It must be somebody obvious but at the same time, for some reason, you would then find that it was *not* obvious, that he could not possibly have done it. But really of course he *had*." What Christie described is the "double bluff," a narrative strategy that makes a false suspect appear guilty (Twist #1) to deflect attention from the real perpetrator, who originally seemed to be falsely accused (Twist #2). It was also in *Styles* that she introduced Hercule Poirot. (More on Poirot later.)

Christie wrote *Styles* between working at the dispensary and taking care of her dying grandmother, Margaret (Grannie B), at Ashfield. However, the novel truly came together in the summer of 1916 when Christie checked into the Moorland Hotel in Dartmoor. For twelve days, she wrote each morning. When she returned home from Dartmoor, she sent the story off to publishers; it would be another four years before *The Mysterious Affair at Styles* was finally released by publisher John Lane at The Bodley Head.

The More You Know

Beginning with *The Mysterious Affair at Styles*, Christie kept notebooks in which she recorded ideas for her novels. Scholar John Curran later assembled the seventy-three extant notebooks for readers. The notebooks are mostly exercise books used by schoolchildren; in fact, some of them had originally belonged to her daughter, Rosalind, before they were commandeered by Agatha. In 2019, Curran published the full collection of these notebooks in *Agatha Christie's Complete Secret Notebooks*.

The Golden Age of Murder

Christie published roughly one-third of her novels during the "Golden Age of Detective Fiction." The term was coined by Marxist politician (and fan of detective fiction) John Strachey, to describe the interwar period (1918–1939) when hundreds of writers in Britain, including Christie, were publishing whodunits. Their audience numbered in the millions, and detective fiction was one of the most popular genres of the era. An estimated 75 percent of this readership was female.

One word that repeatedly comes up in literary discussions of Golden Age detective fiction is "game." In 1928, for example, crime novelist S.S. Van Dine published an article in which he stated, "The detective story is a kind of intellectual game . . . a sporting event." To play the game properly, said Van Dine, writers must adhere to the genre's "very definite laws" and resist such "trickeries" as pinning the crime on a character who is introduced at the last minute. Why? So that readers can solve the case too. To this end, detective novels like Christie's *The Murder of Roger Ackroyd* include visual elements such as floor plans, maps, and handwriting samples for the reader to examine.

Many Golden Age writers also set their crimes in socially enclosed worlds, whether that's Christie's country villages or the upper-class settings of Dorothy L. Sayers's London. Broader political unrest, economic hardship, and the lives of the working classes rarely appear in these novels. Murder gets treated as an eruption in an otherwise peaceful world. These two features—their sporting nature and separation from the real world—contributed to how the era got its name. They are also the reason these stories were criticized by later crime writers like Raymond Chandler.

Christie herself pushed beyond these conventions. By the time she wrote *The Murder of Roger Ackroyd* in 1926, she was exploring new concepts in human psychology, such as PTSD, experimenting with form, and addressing the social changes (more divorces, the "New Woman," escalating taxes on country estates) taking place around her.

THE MORE YOU KNOW

In 1928, S.S. Van Dine devised a list of "Twenty Rules for Writing Detective Stories." The list, half tongue-in-cheek, half serious, includes the rule that "the final pinning of a crime" should never be "on a twin." A year later, Ronald Knox, a Catholic priest, came up with his "Ten Commandments" of detective fiction, including "Not more than one secret room or passage is allowable."

Introducing Hercule Poirot

Seen today as a legendary detective in crime fiction, Hercule Poirot was first described in *The Mysterious Affair at Styles* as an "extraordinary looking little man . . . hardly more than five feet four inches" with a head "exactly the shape of an egg" and a mustache "very stiff and military. . . . I believe a speck of dust would have caused him more pain than a bullet wound."

When she began her first mystery novel in 1916, Christie decided that her detective would be nothing like Sherlock Holmes. While Holmes fits the image of a classic male hero (tall and fit with "remarkable strength," Poirot is characterized as short, overweight, and oldish. He is a "retired" police detective at the end of his career. And while Holmes is British (like his primary readership at the time of publication), Poirot is Belgian.

Poirot is also portrayed in *Styles* and Christie's other stories as a dandy—a common term at the time that referred to a man who was very particular about his appearance. Poirot, for example, takes great care with the crease of his pants, the shine in his shoes, and the flower in his buttonhole. He is also very confident in his abilities, describing himself in *The Mystery of the Blue Train* as "probably the greatest detective in the world." In addition, he is known for having a love of symmetry and for his use of what he calls, in reference to his brain, his "little gray cells."

Often underestimated by others, Poirot uses those assumptions to his advantage. He acts the part of the ignorant foreigner and a man so obsessed with himself that he seemingly notices nothing else. "He was at his most foreign today," the narrator describes him in *Five Little Pigs*, "out to be despised but patronized."

Over time, Christie would grow tired of her character, just as Sir Arthur Conan Doyle reportedly did of Holmes. As she would later write, "There are moments when I have felt: 'Why—Why—Why did I ever invent this detestable, bombastic, tiresome little creature?'" Regardless, Poirot would remain central to her career and popular with readers. Over the course of fifty-five years, he would appear in a total of thirty-three novels, two plays, and over fifty stories by Christie.

THE MORE YOU KNOW

If you follow a strict chronology and assume that Poirot retired from the Belgian police force at age sixty-five, he would have been one hundred and twenty years old by the time of *Curtain*'s publication in 1975. Christie often stated that she made a mistake in making Poirot a "retired officer" in *Styles*. At some point, as she did with Miss Marple, she simply relegated him to an eternal old age.

From Five Little Pigs, Chapter 3

"I am gratified," said Poirot untruly, "that I am so well known to you. My success, let me tell you, has been founded on the psychology—the eternal why? of human behavior. That, M. Blake, is what interests the world in crime today. It used to be romance. Famous crimes were retold from one angle only—the love story connected with them. Nowadays it is very different. People read with interest that Dr. Crippen murdered his wife because she was a big bouncing woman and he was little and insignificant and therefore she made him feel inferior. They read of some famous woman criminal that she killed because she'd been snubbed by her father when she was three years old. It is, as I say, the why of crime that interests nowadays."

Philip Blake said, with a slight yawn:

"The why of most crimes is obvious enough, I should say. Usually money."

Poirot cried:

"Ah, but my dear sir, the why must never be obvious. That is the whole point!"

"And that's where you come in?"

"And that, as you say, is where I come in! It is proposed to rewrite the stories of certain bygone crimes—from the psychological angle. Psychology in crime, it is my specialty. I have accepted the commission."

Philip Blake grinned.

"Pretty lucrative, I suppose?"

"I hope so—I certainly hope so."

Keeping House

In the fall of 1918, Agatha was living at Ashfield with Clara and volunteering at the Torquay hospital, still waiting to hear from publishers about *The Mysterious Affair at Styles*. One afternoon, she got a telegram from her husband, Archie: He'd been posted to the Air Ministry in London. This meant that he was coming home for good, and as Agatha writes, "It was goodbye to Ashfield and the start of my new life, my married life."

Her first task was to find a place to live. As she would later describe, "A year after the armistice, finding anywhere to live was about the most difficult thing in the world. Hundreds of couples were scouring London." Fortunately, she found a place quickly: a flat with "a bed full of large, iron lumps" and a "microscopic kitchenette" on 5 Northwick Terrace in St. John's Wood. Archie's batman, Bartlett, and the general caretaker, Mrs. Woods, who did the "serious cooking," as Agatha would put it, looked after Archie and Agatha. Once settled in her new home, Agatha wrote poems for the literary journal *Poetry of Today* while also taking courses in bookkeeping and shorthand. She also learned how to cook and barter prices with food sellers, remarking later in life that "I'd have made a good maid."

Within two months of living with her husband, Agatha discovered she was pregnant. Archie, seeing no chance for promotion, decided to leave the Air Force and found a job in the city at a comfortable 500 pounds per year. With a baby on the way and a bigger income, they found a new, larger flat with lots of windows and, according to Agatha, "hideous furniture." Agatha bought new furniture and "threw herself heartily into the business of decoration."

On Archie's salary, keeping both a nurse and a maid was difficult, but ever-resourceful Agatha managed to find affordable help. The nurse was "sharp of tongue" Jessie Swannell, who, according to Agatha, loved Rosalind but distrusted Agatha and Archie, and a maid named Rose, who didn't like children or nurses. Rose took the job only after Archie lied to her about having a mutual friend. (As Agatha recalled, the lie was her own idea.)

LITERARY CONNECTIONS

As much as Christie loved finding and decorating homes, her fiction doesn't go into much detail about houses. She once explained in an interview, "I don't like describing people or places, I just want to get on with dialogue." As scholars have pointed out, it is the TV and film versions of Christie's works, especially the BBC's *Miss Marple* series and the ITV series *Agatha Christie's Poirot*, that emphasize cozy or lavish furnishings and decor and garden settings.

Becoming a Mother

Raised in a Victorian household, Agatha would recall having little idea of what pregnancy or childbirth entailed: "My ideas of having a baby had been that they were things that were practically automatic." She didn't understand why, after one of Archie's leaves, she didn't immediately become pregnant. (It took four years—from December 1914 to roughly December 1918—for her to conceive. The cause for this delay isn't clear.)

In her autobiography, Agatha recounts her first visit to pediatrician Dr. Stabb a few months into her pregnancy. He advised coming back to see him a couple of months before the baby was born, "just to see that everything was the right way up." When she complained of morning sickness, Stabb reassured her that it would end soon. In fact, Agatha suffered from morning sickness right up to the day she delivered.

The Christies' first and only child was born on August 5, 1919, weighing 8½ pounds. The child was a girl—Rosalind Margaret Clarissa Christie—and was born at Ashfield with Clara and a midwife in attendance. According to Agatha, Archie was over the moon about having a girl: "Archie was very definite that he must have a daughter" because he thought he'd be "jealous" of a boy.

While Clara had thrown herself into motherhood, Agatha's relationship with her daughter, Rosalind, was distant by all accounts. Agatha herself would say of being a parent that "a child is yours, and yet is mysteriously a stranger. . . . It is like a strange plant which you have brought home. . . ." Christie scholars note that in one sense, Agatha's statement reflects early-twentieth-century ideals about parenthood, which held that children shouldn't be coddled or indulged.

Some biographers suggest that Agatha may have felt Rosalind was more Archie's child than hers. Rosalind resembled Archie more closely than she did Agatha, not only in looks but also in tastes and behavior. Like Archie, Rosalind was practical and realistic, more interested in sports and the outdoors than in made-up stories. Agatha later recounted how quickly father and daughter became a pair; as a child, Rosalind would clean her father's golf clubs and attend him on the golf course while her mother stayed at home writing.

THE MORE YOU KNOW

Child-rearing manuals of the 1910s and 1920s stressed a rigid, disciplinary approach to parenting. New mothers were instructed not to hold their infant unless they were feeding them or otherwise providing basic care. A *Handbook of Obstetric Nursing* (1911), purchased by many middle-class mothers like Agatha, warned parents that those who "foolishly spoil" their children would see them develop into "little tyrants."

The Empire Tour

In 1922, just over two years after Rosalind was born, Archie was growing bored with his job when a new opportunity arose. An old schoolmaster of his, Major Ernest Belcher, was organizing a tour to promote the British Empire Exhibition. Scheduled to open in Wembley Park in 1924, the exhibition was designed not only to showcase British products and inventions but also to boost trade between Britain and other countries. The tour would cover South Africa, Australia, New Zealand, Hawaii, and Canada, and Archie's job would be as financial advisor. For a fee, Belcher offered Archie 1,000 pounds plus all expenses paid and invited Agatha to join.

The trip meant leaving two-year-old Rosalind in the care of Clara and Madge. While Madge tried to dissuade Agatha from going, citing Rosalind (and Monty's recent return home—more on this later), Clara insisted she do so. According to Agatha, she told her younger daughter, "Remember, if you're not with your husband, if you leave him too much, *you'll lose him*."

The couple accepted, setting sail on January 20, 1922, in a ship called the *Kildonan Castle*. Photos would show them swimming at Sea Point, eating oranges at Yanga, and purchasing wooden giraffes for Rosalind in Cape Town along the tour.

But the trip had its difficulties. Belcher, whom Agatha would refer to as "Wild Man," had become explosive, mean, and full of himself. (Agatha would later base Sir Eustace Pedler, the villain in her 1924 novel, *The Man in the Brown Suit,* on Belcher.) There were also many social events to attend, where she was sometimes treated coldly. On one of these occasions, she sat up front with the male dignitaries—and was harshly reprimanded by a wife who told her to move to the back. At various points in the trip, both Archie and Agatha became ill—Agatha with seasickness, Archie with his perpetual stomach troubles.

The couple returned home on December 1, 1922. While they were gone, Christie's second detective novel, *The Secret Adversary,* which she had written the year before, had been published by The Bodley Head. What's more, the first installment of *The Murder on the Links,* her second novel featuring Poirot, was soon to appear in the December 2022 issue of *The Grand Magazine.*

The More You Know

A five-part documentary TV series called *Travels with Agatha Christie & Sir David Suchet* aired in the US in March 2025. Suchet, whom many people believe embodies Hercule Poirot, visits the places Agatha and Archie toured in 1922.

From The Man in the Brown Suit, Chapter 9

Sir Eustace turned suddenly.

"Very clever. Very creditable. But I've still a word to say. If I've lost the trick, so have you. You'll never be able to bring the murder of Nadina home to me. I was in Marlow on that day, that's all you've got against me. No one can prove that I even knew the woman. But you knew her, you had a motive for killing her and your record's against you. You're a thief, remember, a thief. There's one thing you don't know, perhaps. *I've got the diamonds.* And here goes—"

With an incredibly swift movement, he stooped, swung up his arm and threw. There was a tinkle of breaking glass, as the object went through the window and disappeared into the blazing mass opposite.

"There goes your only hope of establishing your innocence over the Kimberley affair. And now we'll talk. I'll drive a bargain with you. You've got me cornered. Race will find all he needs in this house. There's a chance for me if I get away. I'm done for if I stay, but so are you, young man! There's a skylight in the next room. A couple of minutes' start and I shall be all right. I've got one or two little arrangements all ready made. You let me out that way, and give me a start—and I'll leave you a signed confession that I killed Nadina."

"Yes, Harry," I cried. "Yes, yes, yes!"

"No, Anne, a thousand times, no. You don't know what you're saying."

"I do. It solves everything."

"I'd never be able to look Race in the face again. I'll take my chance, but I'm damned if I'll let this slippery old fox get away. It's no good, Anne. I won't do it."

Sir Eustace chuckled. He accepted defeat without the least emotion.

"Well, well," he remarked. "You seem to have both met your master, Anne. But I can assure you both that moral rectitude does not always pay."

Agatha Christie, World Traveler

During her year on the "Empire Tour," Agatha wrote what she called a "diary" of letters to her mother. Clara kept all these letters, and when she died, Agatha reclaimed them. Later collected in a book edited by Agatha's grandson, Mathew Prichard, these letters provide a close look at Agatha as a traveler, from what she enjoyed to what frustrated her.

Agatha wrote often, for example, of the women she encountered on the tour. One letter recounts her meeting with the "Champion lady runner" of Australia (Mrs. Baddock). Agatha took a photo of Baddock smiling in her running outfit of bloomers and a cap just as she was about to take off in a race. Agatha also recalls the female members of the Bell family, who owned a massive farm in Queensland. "Mrs. Bell is delightful, full of character . . . All her children adore her. . . . They [the girls] are all mad on horses and go about all day in shirts and breeches."

Agatha's letters home also detail her observations of nature along the journey, including Lake Louise, Table Mountain, Victoria Falls, and Waddamana in Tasmania. Of Waddamana, she wrote: "All Australian scenery that I have seen has a faintly austere quality, the distance is all a soft blue green—sometimes almost grey. . . . And here and there great clumps of trees have been ringbarked and have died, and then they are ghost trees, all white, with white waving branches."

Fans can learn about her adventures and discoveries throughout these letters: "I never knew what a banana could be," she wrote after visiting a plantation in Honolulu. On a trip to a chocolate factory in Melbourne, she described the variety of cocoa beans from Trinidad, Ceylon, West Africa, and New Guinea. And in South Africa, New Zealand, and Honolulu, she enjoyed surfing: "Oh, the moment of complete triumph, on the day that I kept my balance and came right into shore standing upright on my board!"

Ultimately, Agatha would spend much of her life abroad, and travel would be a big part of many of her novels, from *Murder on the Orient Express* (1934) and *Three Act Tragedy* (1934) to *Appointment with Death* (1938) and *A Caribbean Mystery* (1964).

The More You Know

Agatha was one of the first British women to ride a surfboard standing up. After her first attempt at surfing in South Africa, she kept at the sport, developing her skills in New Zealand and later in Honolulu, where she rode a surfboard named Fred.

Tommy and Tuppence

Portrayed as stylish, witty, and nonchalant about danger, Tommy and Tuppence Beresford are a married couple who dabble in sleuthing. And as Christie would later describe, their characters were pure enjoyment to write.

Launched in 1922 with *The Secret Adversary,* Tommy and Tuppence are a double act, characterized by complementary traits: Tuppence is portrayed as intuitive and plucky, while Tommy is cautious and logical. Tuppence, however, is shown to be the superior spy. The five books in which the couple appears—*The Secret Adversary, Partners in Crime* (1929), *N or M?* (1941), *By the Pricking of My Thumbs* (1968), and *Postern of Fate* (1973)—"each regale readers with adventure" (the dedication in *The Secret Adversary* reads, "To all those who lead monotonous lives in the hope that they may experience at second hand the delights and dangers of adventure"). The books feature criminal gangs, undercover work, national intelligence, and Nazis.

In *The Secret Adversary,* Tommy and Tuppence are childhood friends down on their luck when they meet accidentally in London and decide to team up. Their job: to solve problems. "Two young adventurers for hire," their ad in the newspapers states. "Willing to do anything, go anywhere.

Pay must be good." They soon become involved in international espionage and fall in love by the novel's end.

At the beginning of *N or M?*, written sometime during 1939 and 1940, Tommy and Tuppence are a middle-aged couple with grown children. They wish to join the war effort but are considered too old for active intelligence work. Through a series of ingeniously sneaky steps, they become involved in a counterespionage mission that involves a seaside hotel, a fifth column (a group of people who betray their country by collaborating with its enemies), and a decoy toddler.

As the series progresses, Tommy and Tuppence, unlike Poirot or Miss Marple, age in real time. (In *Postern of Fate*, they are grandparents!) The couple never acquired the traction of Poirot or Marple, but Christie loved these characters, regarding them as a welcome break from writing detective fiction.

THE MORE YOU KNOW

After reading *N or M?*, MI5 (the UK's domestic security and counterterrorism agency) suspected Christie of having a spy in the government. The reason was that she named one of her characters Major Bletchley, a character who repeatedly boasts that he knows the secrets of Britain's wartime efforts. Christie was friends with a code breaker named Dilly Knox, who worked as part of a team at Bletchley Park, the center during World War II of cryptanalysis (code breaking) of the Axis powers. M15 suspected that Knox gave Christie classified information.

The Man Behind the Woman

It had taken Christie four years and six rejections before she published her first detective novel, *The Mysterious Affair at Styles,* with John Lane of The Bodley Head in 1920. By her own account, the firm treated her shabbily. In addition to sitting on the novel for two years, Lane issued a contract that included no advance, 10 percent of royalties on sales over two thousand copies, and a stipulation that the firm would receive half of anything the book earned from serial or dramatic rights. The contract also stipulated that Christie produce an additional four books for which The Bodley Head would be given first right of refusal.

But things changed in 1923, not long after she and her husband returned from their international tour. Now with three published novels (*Styles, The Secret Adversary,* and *The Murder on the Links*), she was paid 500 pounds (about 26,000 pounds today) by the *London Evening News* to serialize her upcoming book, *The Man in the Brown Suit.*

In the wake of this success, Christie visited Hughes Massie, the literary agency that Eden Phillpotts had once recommended to her. There, she met Edmund Cork, who would become her agent for the next fifty years. His vision for Christie's career included serial rights, American publications, and film adaptations. "I placed myself in his hands, unreservedly, and left his office with a sigh of relief," she would write.

From the start, Cork negotiated tough deals for his client. His first step was to extricate Christie from her contract with The Bodley Head, proposing to them that with her growing fame, Christie should get an advance of 200 pounds per book. According to Christie biographer Janet Morgan, John Lane told Cork that anyone who would pay that much was welcome to Christie's books. Agatha was free (though she did have to deliver on two more novels for The Bodley Head first).

Over the next five decades, Cork would advise Christie on book advances, taxes, adaptations, radio productions, and serial rights. He would supply her with what she needed for her archaeological trips to the Middle East, defend her against charges of fraud and anti-Semitism, and devise a plan for saving her struggling financial situation. His office would deliver on all her requests, from the small to the lavish. They would also agree to her blanket refusal to do book signings.

THE MORE YOU KNOW

When talking about all Edmund Cork did for her, Christie called it the "Cork service." In addition to his tasks as her literary agent, he also managed her tenants, made flight arrangements and foreign currency transactions, booked hotels and tickets, and even placed bets for her at horse races, according to Laura Thompson.

The House of Collins

William Collins (now HarperCollins) in the UK was one of two publishers Agatha Christie would have throughout most of her career (the second being Dodd, Mead & Co. in the US). By the end of the 1920s, once Agatha had joined William Collins, she was the publisher's most famous author. And as the years progressed, its head, William ("Billy") Collins, instructed his staff to provide her with whatever she requested, whether it was a Dictaphone, a new typewriter, or a certain brand of maple syrup she'd once had in America. In 1953, he even bought her a car, a Humber Super Snipe. He wanted to get her a Jaguar, but as she later recalled, she protested that she was "too old" to have such a "fun" vehicle.

However, Agatha also felt William Collins didn't always pay her the attention or respect they should. In 1939, she would become furious when she learned that an item in the forthcoming *Crime Club News*, put out by Collins, was about to summarize the plot of *And Then There Were None*, even though she had repeatedly expressed her dislike of such summaries. She would also complain from time to time about publicity blurbs and book cover designs: "The pinky color was more sentimental than murderous!" Edits made by the publisher to fix grammar and spelling were also frustrating to the author. "Perhaps you would make it clear," she wrote to Billy Collins, "*not* to change the spelling of the author unless it is actually misspelt. If I prefer phantasy to fantasy (both words are in dictionary) I want it left alone. . . . I don't want sentences twisted around to be more grammatical when they are part of someone's spoken conversation." She and Collins occasionally fought over titles too; for one book, she wanted the title to be *Remembered Death*, while he preferred *Sparkling Cyanide*. Collins won the argument.

Despite the disagreements and frustrations, Christie and Billy Collins would enjoy a close friendship throughout the years. In 1966, Christie would give a handwritten note to her longtime publisher, thanking him for a party that he threw upon the publication of a book by her second husband, Max Mallowan. "As you know I am usually not a party woman," she wrote. "But it really did feel all friends together." In 1958, she would dedicate *Ordeal by Innocence* "To Billy Collins with affection and gratitude."

LITERARY CONNECTIONS

One of Agatha's favorite novels, *Ordeal by Innocence*, got mixed reviews when it came out in 1958. Some critics felt it lacked the strong focus and structure of her other works, while a few complained that the novel read too much like a psychological thriller, *The Observer* saying that the "serious socio-psychological approach doesn't suit" Christie's writing.

Changes at Home

While Agatha was finding success in publishing, Archie returned from the Empire Tour unemployed. His former London position had been given to someone else while he was away. Once home, he spent weeks looking for work, which, as Agatha recounted, made him irritable and depressed.

Christie biographers speculate that there may have been deeper reasons for Archie's depression. Having fought in the war, he may have been suffering from shell shock—a state of psychological distress resulting from trauma. If so, Archie never talked about the war to Agatha: "His one idea in those days was to forget such things." Lacking a job, Archie also had to face Clara with a sense of having failed her daughter and granddaughter, as Laura Thompson suggests. And while he referred to Agatha as his "clever wife," his own sense of failure may have been compounded by her career success.

Archie eventually found a job in finance at Austral Development Ltd., estate agents, sometime in 1923. Agatha, meanwhile, got back to writing. In 1924, she published *The Man in the Brown Suit*, a novel set in South Africa featuring a female sleuth, secret codes, and stolen diamonds. Following this publication, she still had one book left in her contract with The Bodley Head: *The Secret of Chimneys*, which follows a male drifter who gets entangled in an international conspiracy that involves a lost diamond hidden at the Chimneys estate. It was published in 1925. Meanwhile, her stories were appearing in popular venues such as *The Sketch* and the newly launched *Flynn's Weekly*, a detective magazine.

Now with more financial security, the Christies decided to move to Sunningdale, a posh London suburb with a highly rated golf course. They considered a house that, as Agatha described, was "a sort of millionaire-style Savoy suite transferred to the country." It also had a reputation for being unlucky: The first couple who lived there went bankrupt, the second owner lost his wife, and the third couple divorced. Archie and Agatha bought the home nonetheless and renamed it Styles, the country house setting of Agatha's first novel—and scene of a murder.

THE MORE YOU KNOW

With the money she earned from serializing *The Man in the Brown Suit*, Agatha bought herself a car, a gray Morris Cowley. "Oh the joy that car was to me!" she would later write. "To be able to go anywhere you chose; to places beyond the reach of your legs—it widened your whole horizon." According to the British Motor Museum, on average only 12 percent of British women applied for a driver's license during the 1920s; only 3 percent owned their own car.

The Murder of Roger Ackroyd

It was 1925; Agatha had been married for eleven years and writing detective fiction for nine years. Having finished her contract with The Bodley Head, she was now free to write her first novel for William Collins. This novel turned out to be *The Murder of Roger Ackroyd*, her most controversial work, published in June 1926.

Christie hinged her mystery on an uncommon plot twist. Spoiler alert: The narrator, Dr. James Sheppard, turns out to be the murderer. In fact, the story unfolds as Sheppard's manuscript, written as the chronicle of what he believes will be Poirot's one and only failure.

"I got hold of a formula there," Christie would write about *Ackroyd.* Next to Sir Arthur Conan Doyle killing off Sherlock Holmes in "The Final Problem," no detective writer up to this point had delivered such a shocking twist. It catapulted Christie to global celebrity.

The New York Times Book Review stated that "Miss Christie is not only an expert technician and a remarkably good story-teller, but she knows . . . just the right number of hints to offer as to the real murderer." The *Daily Sketch* thought *Ackroyd* the "best thriller ever." Not everyone offered praise, however. The *News Chronicle* called the novel a "tasteless and unfortunate let-down by a writer we had grown to admire." One reader was reportedly so angry about the ending that he proposed "in the future not to buy any more of her books."

In response to the criticism that she "cheated" in writing *Ackroyd* with an unreliable narrator, Agatha said that while lying to readers is wrong, withholding information from them isn't (though she stipulated that a careful reader of *Ackroyd* could find all the clues they needed to solve the murder). And despite the critics, *Ackroyd* sold out of its first five thousand copies within weeks. The book also landed Christie squarely in the realm of what scholars call the "feminine middlebrow": novels written by women and aimed at a middle-class female readership. By 1926, detective fiction had become highly popular among women, addressing such topics as domestic abuse and unwanted pregnancy.

LITERARY CONNECTIONS

The 1920s and 1930s were filled with female detective writers, among them the "Queens of Crime," as pop culture dubbed them. But there were many other, lesser-known female detective writers, including Patricia Wentworth, the author of thirty-two whodunits featuring a retired governess who becomes a professional private detective. There was also Gladys Mitchell, who published a total of sixty-six crime novels in which a female psychoanalyst solves crimes, and Mildred Wirt Benson, who launched the Nancy Drew books in 1930.

From The Murder of Roger Ackroyd, Chapter 27

Five a.m. I am very tired—but I have finished my task. My arm aches from writing.

A strange end to my manuscript. I meant it to be published some day as the history of one of Poirot's failures! Odd, how things pan out. . . .

My greatest fear all through has been Caroline. I have fancied she might guess. Curious the way she spoke that day of my "strain of weakness."

Well, she will never know the truth. There is, as Poirot said, one way out. . . .

I can trust him. He and Inspector Raglan will manage it between them. I should not like Caroline to know. She is fond of me, and then, too, she is proud. . . . My death will be a grief to her, but grief passes. . . .

When I have finished writing, I shall enclose this whole manuscript in an envelope and address it to Poirot.

Queens of Crime

There were four leading figures among Golden Age detective writers: Agatha Christie, Dorothy L. Sayers, Margery Allingham, and Ngaio Marsh, otherwise known as the "Queens of Crime." In 1923, Sayers created Lord Peter Wimsey, an aristocrat who also solves crimes as an amateur detective. Wimsey embodies Golden Age detective fiction, approaching crime as a game. Sayers's most acclaimed novels are *Strong Poison* (1930), about an author accused of murdering her husband, and *Gaudy Night* (1935), which introduced Harriet Vane, the woman who would become Wimsey's wife and partner in crime solving.

Margery Allingham's detective, Albert Campion, appeared in eighteen novels and over twenty stories. Over the course of these works, he matures to a serious intelligence officer. Allingham's most acclaimed novels are *More Work for the Undertaker* (1948), about a family who lives among a network of gangsters, and *The Tiger in the Smoke* (1952), about a war widow who discovers her presumed-dead husband may be alive.

Ngaio Marsh introduced her detective, Roderick Alleyn, a Metropolitan Police officer, in her 1934 novel, *A Man Lay Dead*. She would eventually publish a total of thirty-two detective novels featuring Alleyn. Marsh's most acclaimed novels are *A Man Lay Dead*, concerning a killing while guests are playing a parlor game of Murder, and *Artists in Crime* (1938), in which an artist's model is brutally murdered.

Crime scholars highlight the different strengths of the Queens of Crime: Sayers's wit, stylish prose, and game-like approach to crime; Allingham's "precisely observed characters," as *Guardian* critic Jane Stevenson puts it; Marsh's realistic social settings and character observations; and Christie's clever misdirections and plot twists. Christie's favorite detective writer, however, was someone else: the American novelist Elizabeth Daly, who, at age sixty-two, published her debut novel, *Unexpected Night*, in 1940. The novel explores the suspicious death of a young, wealthy invalid on his twenty-first birthday. Apparently, Christie appreciated how Daly's novels, in contrast to the hard-boiled school of crime writing, eschewed gritty realism for a cozier, more genteel approach to crime.

LITERARY CONNECTIONS

In 2025, writer Marie Benedict published her novel *The Queens of Crime*. Set in London, 1930, it follows fictitious versions of Christie, Dorothy L. Sayers, Ngaio Marsh, Margery Allingham, and Baroness Emma Orczy (who wrote *The Scarlet Pimpernel*) as they show off their detective skills to the male members of London's Detection Club.

Heartbroken

On April 5, 1926, Clara Miller passed away. As Agatha recounts, she was on a train to Abney Hall when suddenly she sensed the moment of Clara's death: "I felt a *coldness*, as though I was invaded all over, from head to feet, with some deadly chill—and I thought: '*Mother is dead*.'" According to Agatha, Clara shared a psychic connection with her children, especially her youngest. She seemed to always know what Agatha was feeling, and Agatha would later describe the "wonderful relief when somebody knows what's in your mind . . . so that you are at last released from that long bondage of silence." This time, however, it was Agatha who knew.

When Agatha returned from the Grand Tour in December 1922, she had noticed a decline in her mother. Clara moved awkwardly, seemed less patient with the staff at Ashfield, and was more forgetful in general. Then, at other times, she would seem herself again. This alternation between low and high points continued for a few years until Clara came down with a severe case of bronchitis in 1926. Madge then arranged for Clara to stay at Abney Hall, the grand but gloomy estate owned by the Watts family, which Madge had married into in 1902. Madge notified Agatha, who then got a train to see her mother. Unfortunately, Clara died that same day—a few hours before Agatha made it to Abney.

Agatha later described her grief over the loss and how it was compounded by Archie's inability to provide emotional support. "He had a violent dislike of illness, death, and trouble of any kind," she said. Archie invited Agatha to accompany him to Spain, where he had business to conduct, but she refused, noting that Clara's estate needed attention.

She left London with six-year-old Rosalind to undertake the task of clearing out her mother's house in Ashfield. By her account, weeks passed at Ashfield with little word from her husband. During this time, she couldn't sleep and hardly ate.

Archie eventually came to Ashfield that August for Rosalind's seventh birthday, and seemed to Agatha to be a very different man . . .

LITERARY CONNECTIONS

In *Unfinished Portrait,* the heroine, Celia, is shattered by her mother's death. The novel describes Celia's "gallant little mother," whom she had always regarded as "wonderful and satisfying . . . And now her mother had gone. . . . The bottom had fallen out of Celia's world."

A Real Secret Adversary

As Agatha would recall, when Archie arrived at Ashfield in August 1926, "He went through the motions of ordinary greetings, but he was, quite simply, *not Archie*." The couple was supposed to leave for Italy that month, for a short getaway to lift Agatha's spirits. But Archie hadn't bought the tickets or even made plans. Instead, he told her, "I'd like you to give me a divorce," explaining that he had fallen in love with a woman named Nancy Neele.

Nancy was twenty-seven—nine years younger than Agatha—and the divorce meant the end of a twelve-year marriage. At first, Agatha "thought it was something that would pass." But once the family was back at Styles a week or so later, Archie left for his gentlemen's club in London. Agatha blamed herself, remembering Clara's advice to never let her husband feel neglected. During this time, she became distraught and ill. Her assistant, Charlotte ("Carlo") Fisher, who had been visiting family in Yorkshire, returned to Styles to find that Agatha wasn't sleeping or eating.

After a few weeks, Archie came back to Styles for Rosalind's sake, but soon reaffirmed his desire to leave. He had grown impatient with Agatha's grief over Clara's death and wanted someone who'd be attentive and fun. "I did tell you once, long ago, that I hate it when people are ill or unhappy—it sort of spoils everything for me," he said to Agatha. In Nancy Neele, Christie biographers speculate, Archie saw a young woman who would be a cheerful, easy companion.

On Friday, December 3, 1926, as Agatha was dining alone at Styles, Archie sent a message to say he was spending the weekend with friends in Godalming. Nancy Neele was among those friends. That night, Agatha wrote two letters, one to Carlo and one to Archie. At about 9:45 p.m., once Rosalind was asleep, she packed a suitcase and left home in her Morris Cowley.

The More You Know

Functioning as "second homes" for men, gentlemen's clubs such as the one Archie Christie and Agatha's father, Frederick, went to were a staple of nineteenth- and early-twentieth-century London. They were homosocial spaces, designed to foster friendships among men. Private and expensive, they typically included a library, study, game and billiard rooms, bathrooms, and bedrooms. At the height of their popularity in the 1890s, there were an estimated four hundred gentlemen's clubs in London.

Disappearing Act

A police report stated that Agatha's car was found on Saturday, December 4. It was located in a nature preserve named Newlands Corner outside the town of Guildford, near a lake ominously called the "Silent Pool." The first person to find the car was a fifteen-year-old "gypsy lad" named George Best, who said the car's lights were still on and a back door was open. Inside were a woman's fur coat; a packed, open suitcase; an attaché case; and an expired driver's license issued in the name of Mrs. Agatha Christie.

Biographer Gillian Gill describes Agatha's disappearance as "the one dramatic act of her life." Despite her growing fame, Agatha lived a relatively quiet existence until this vanishing. And as Laura Thompson suggests, "Something of the mystery will always remain." Police files were destroyed during World War II, and Agatha never wrote about her disappearance or allowed anyone to speak of it in her presence. Those close to the author never commented publicly about the incident.

Her autobiography also gives little detail about the disappearance, though she writes that she "was at this time in a very despondent state of mind. I just wanted my life to end." According to newspaper reports, she drove through much of the night, skirting Godalming, until her car stalled at about 6 a.m. A farmhand found her in a "frenzied condition" around 6:30 a.m. He got the car to start for her, but before he could offer to help her further, Agatha headed off. She drove down a slope until her Morris Cowley car slammed into some hedges, and she hit her head on the steering wheel. Exiting the car, she took nothing with her but her black handbag. "Up to this moment I was Mrs. Christie," she later wrote. Now, she would become someone else.

LITERARY CONNECTIONS

Many writers and filmmakers have dramatized Agatha Christie's disappearance. The first was Kathleen Tynan, in a 1978 novel called *Agatha*. A year later, *Agatha*, a film adaptation of the book starring Vanessa Redgrave, was released. Other dramatizations include the film *Agatha and the Truth of Murder* (2018), in which the novelist solves the case of a missing woman during her disappearance, and the novel *The Mystery of Mrs. Christie* (2020), which imagines the disappearance through Agatha's and Archie's eyes.

From The Mystery of the Blue Train, Chapter 36

"Trains are relentless things, aren't they, Monsieur Poirot? People are murdered and die, but they go on just the same. I am talking nonsense, but you know what I mean."

"Yes, yes, I know. Life is like a train, Mademoiselle. It goes on. And it is a good thing that that is so."

"Why?"

"Because the train gets to its journey's end at last, and there is a proverb about that in your language, Mademoiselle."

"'Journey's end in lovers meeting.'" Lenox laughed. "That is not going to be true for me."

"Yes—yes, it is true. You are young, younger than you yourself know. Trust the train, Mademoiselle, for it is *le bon Dieu* who drives it."

The whistle of the engine came again.

"Trust the train, Mademoiselle," murmured Poirot again. "And trust Hercule Poirot. He knows."

Mrs. Teresa Neele of Cape Town

The morning after her disappearance, while police were investigating her abandoned car, Agatha went to Clandon station, where she took a train to Waterloo station in London. There, she bought some toiletries and a coat at an Army and Navy store, then took a taxi to the department store Harrods. At Harrods, she dropped off a ring to be repaired, asking that they send it to Mrs. Neele at the Harrogate Hydropathic Hotel, called the "Hydro," in Yorkshire (Neele being the last name of Archie's mistress, Nancy).

Later that Saturday, Agatha posted a letter to Archie's brother, Campbell, which would resurface later in the mystery of her disappearance. Once at King's Cross station, Agatha took a train for Harrogate and checked into the Hydro on the evening of December 4. She signed the hotel register as "Mrs. Teresa Neele of Capetown, S.A.," spending the next ten days there.

According to reports, Agatha slept in late and had breakfast in bed the following Sunday morning. On Monday, she went into town and bought a new set of clothes, including a pink georgette dress, which she wore that night. She visited the local library, where she checked out a clutch of mystery novels. She also lunched at a local restaurant, took a walk, and conversed with some of the other hotel guests at dinner. And so went the rest of the week, with more shopping trips and luncheons out. During the day, she read and worked crossword puzzles, and in the evenings, she chatted with other guests, played billiards, listened to the hotel band, and even danced with another guest.

Meanwhile, the search for Agatha Christie launched.

THE MORE YOU KNOW

Incorporated in 1871, Army and Navy stores originated as a co-op for military personnel and their families. Goods of all kinds—clothing, groceries, home furnishings—could be purchased at retail prices at these London stores. By the turn of the century, they were open to the public and had expanded to cities like Karachi and Calcutta. Agatha would often go to the Army and Navy store in London accompanied by her grandmother, Auntie-Grannie.

The Letter

By all accounts, Agatha had always been close to her brother-in-law Campbell Christie. The letter she sent him on December 4 explained that she was leaving home to stay at a spa in Yorkshire but didn't provide any more details about where she would be.

Campbell received and read the letter, though he didn't bring it to police attention until the following Wednesday, December 8. Apparently, he hadn't thought anything about it until he'd heard on Monday, December 6, that his sister-in-law was missing. By then, he had lost the letter. When Campbell made a statement to the police and press, he had to rely on his memory of the letter's contents. The *Daily Mail* quoted him as saying, "She [Agatha] was going to a Yorkshire spa to stay with friends and to recuperate."

The detective in charge of the Christie case, Superintendent William Kenward of the Surrey Constabulary, didn't believe that Agatha had written the letter nor gone to a spa. In his view, she was either wandering about the countryside, or she had been killed by her husband. Kenward considered the second possibility more likely.

According to Lucy Worsley, Superintendent William Kenward was a good and dedicated policeman. However, he had "an unhelpful weakness for drama." Until this time, Kenward had enjoyed a long and distinguished career in the police force. But the extent and cost of his manhunt (more on this soon), as well as his failure to locate Agatha earlier in Yorkshire, led to a lot of criticism. He was attacked in the press and had to report personally to the Home Secretary, William Joynson-Hicks, to explain his handling of the case.

LITERARY CONNECTIONS

Letters play a key role in many Christie novels. In *The Moving Finger* (1942), poison-pen letters wreak havoc in an English village. *The A.B.C. Murders* (1936) features a serial killer who sends Poirot letters as clues to his upcoming murders. In *And Then There Were None* (1939), nine of the ten suspects receive a letter inviting them to a gathering at a remote seaside location.

The Manhunt

In the ten days following Agatha's disappearance, Kenward ordered a search of the hills around Newlands Corner, where Christie's car was found. He enlisted the police forces of both Surrey and Berkshire for this search, and soon he had hundreds of volunteers looking for Agatha too. Under Kenward's orders, the nearby Silent Pool was dragged.

As each day passed, the search for Agatha grew more intense, with nearly fifteen thousand citizens volunteering to help find the writer. Among them was crime novelist Dorothy L. Sayers, who combed the area with her husband. Sir Arthur Conan Doyle, who had a decades-long interest in spiritualism, gave one of Agatha's gloves to a medium. (He and Agatha had never met, but Doyle liked and respected Agatha's writing, and he wanted to help.)

Press coverage of the manhunt was extensive. In the words of Gillian Gill, "Reporters besieged Styles, plagued anyone involved in the case for interviews, haunted the police headquarters of two counties, and dogged the steps of those engaged in the investigation." The *Daily News* offered a reward of 100 pounds to anyone who could provide information about the case. Meanwhile, the *Daily Mirror* did a full-page spread on Agatha's disappearance, including photos of police searching the countryside with bloodhounds. The *Daily Mail* engaged crime writers to share their views on the disappearance, which detective novelist Edgar Wallace called "a typical case of 'mental reprisal' on someone who has hurt her."

On Friday, Dec. 10, the *Daily Mail* interviewed Archie Christie. He suggested that Agatha had deliberately disappeared, telling a reporter, "My wife had discussed the possibility of disappearing at will . . . probably for the purpose of her work." News of his relationship with Nancy Neele had begun to surface, and Archie was increasingly being treated as a suspect; by all accounts, he tried to deflect attention away from himself by raising the possibility that Agatha staged her own disappearance. Following this interview, several newspapers attacked Agatha, portraying her as a devious woman who was wasting public money and police resources.

LITERARY CONNECTIONS

In Christie's novel *Sad Cypress* (1940), Elinor Carlisle loves a man whose head has been turned by a much younger woman, Mary Gerrard. "They would have been together here—now," Elinor thinks, "walking side by side in gentle proprietary pleasure, happy—yes, happy together—but for the fatal accident of a girl's wild beauty."

The Mystery

The search for Agatha Christie ended on Tuesday, December 14, when two hotel musicians called the Surrey police that morning to say Agatha was staying at the Hydro. Informed of this news, Archie took the 1:40 train from King's Cross station to Harrogate, arriving at the hotel in the evening. He waited in the lounge, police officers stationed in the corners, until Agatha came down for dinner in what newspapers later described as a "handsome mauve gown."

The hotel was filled with journalists waiting to see what would happen. There were no arguments or tears; the couple simply went into the hotel's lounge to have dinner together. Afterward, Agatha returned to her room. The next morning, followed closely by the press, Archie and Agatha snuck out the hotel's back entrance; got into Madge's waiting car; and boarded a train for Cheadle, where they stayed at Abney Hall, Archie for a few days, Agatha a few weeks.

This marked the end of the eleven-day disappearance of the "Lady Novelist," as newspapers called her. But the question of why Agatha Christie went to Harrogate—and remained there when thousands of people were looking for her—continues to be debated. The official answer, given by Archie that Tuesday evening in a statement to the *Yorkshire Press*, was amnesia: "She has suffered from the most complete loss of memory, and I do not think she knows who she is."

In his book *Agatha Christie and the Eleven Missing Days*, writer Jared Cade argues that Agatha did engineer her disappearance to disrupt her husband's time with Nancy—and that once the situation had escalated, she felt too humiliated to come forward. Other writers have speculated that partial amnesia is the real explanation or that Agatha experienced a dissociative fugue, a condition involving a lapse of identity.

In February 1928, Agatha gave an interview about her disappearance in the *Daily Mail*, in which she admitted wanting to kill herself: "There came into my mind the thought of driving into it" [the pond at Newlands Corner], she said. "However, as my daughter was with me in the car, I dismissed the idea at once. That night I felt terribly miserable. I felt that I could go on no longer. I left home that night in a state of high nervous strain with the intention of doing something desperate." After this interview, Agatha almost never spoke about the incident again—not to friends, acquaintances, or the press.

THE MORE YOU KNOW

The concept of psychogenic amnesia (amnesia caused by psychological rather than physical trauma) developed in the late nineteenth and early twentieth centuries. By all accounts, the first formal case reports of psychogenic amnesia appeared around 1935: nine years after Agatha's disappearance.

"Things Went Too Well"

Biographers note that on one level, Archie's desire for a divorce was straightforward: He fell in love with another, younger woman. "By 1923 Agatha was no longer the beautiful woman of earlier years," Gillian Gill observes. Based on the portrait of marriage in Christie's autobiographical novel, *Unfinished Portrait*, Agatha's changed looks made a difference to Archie.

But Agatha would later recall the couple's complacency as part of why the marriage ended: "We had been through so much worry since we came back from our world tour that it seemed wonderful to enter on this halcyon period. Perhaps it was then that I ought to have felt misgiving. Things went too well. Archie had the work he enjoyed. . . . He had what he had always wanted, to belong to a first-class golf club, and to play every weekend. My writing was going well."

Archie was making an increasingly good living, and the Christie family was enjoying a prosperous life at Styles. But his work in London wasn't as exciting as aviation, which had been the dream of his youth. And while Agatha's writing was "going well," she found Sunningdale "dull" and "pretentious."

Agatha also felt that her marriage to Archie lacked companionship. "I missed the early companionship of our time together . . . the weekends when we had gone by bus or train and had explored places," she would recall. Now, Archie spent the weekday hours in London earning money, and on weekends he played golf—leaving Agatha and Rosalind alone. When she would suggest that they invite their friends from London for a weekend, he'd resist. And when Agatha suggested that they have another child, he said no. "I don't want anyone but Rosalind. . . . And anyway," he added, "there's lots of time."

Later reflecting on the marriage, Agatha never said that she'd been mistaken in marrying Archie Christie. In *A Murder Is Announced*, the character Belle Goedler says, "It's never a mistake to marry a man you want to marry—even if you regret it." Biographers claim this line in the novel reflects Agatha's personal philosophy that it's better to feel passionately, and to take risks, than to lead a life of security.

LITERARY CONNECTIONS

Dull marriages are a common trope in Christie's fiction. In "The Case of the Discontented Husband" (1932), the wife is bored with her husband's routine of tennis and golf. In *Murder in Mesopotamia* (1936), Louise Leidner feels restless with her kindly, devoted husband and is led to commit murder. And in *The Hollow* (1946), Dr. John Christow is bored with his wife and has an affair that results in his own murder.

From 4:50 from Paddington, Chapter 8

"It's a difficult sort of world, isn't it? To get your bearings in, I mean. You see, one hasn't been trained for it."

Lucy recalled what she had heard from Emma.

"You were a fighter pilot, weren't you?" she said. "You've got a D.F.C" [Distinguished Flying Cross]

"That's the sort of thing that puts you all wrong. You've got a gong [slang for a D.F.C.] and so people try to make it easy for you. Give you a job and all that. Very decent of them. But they're all admin jobs, and one simply isn't any good at that sort of thing. Sitting at a desk getting tangled up in figures."

Divorce

When Agatha married Archie, she regarded marriage as a sacrament and divorce to be a sin. Returning from Harrogate, she still hoped that she and Archie would remain married. But things changed significantly over the next two years. After her disappearance, she went to live with Madge while Archie put Styles up for sale. Although Agatha objected, Madge insisted her sister seek psychiatric treatment. Along with Carlo and Rosalind, Agatha moved into a London flat and, by all accounts, likely saw a specialist named William Brown, who specialized in amnesia. The details aren't known, but Brown would have treated patients like Agatha with hypnosis and a "talking cure," where the patient, through conversation, comes to an understanding of their past.

Meanwhile, public criticism of Agatha was intense. News articles described her as a bad mother, a terrible wife, and a hysterical woman who took revenge on her husband and exposed her personal drama to public view. Madge's husband, James Watts, and Archie's brother, Campbell Christie, along with her assistant, Carlo, told Agatha that there would be no reconciliation with Archie and that he loved Nancy. Even seven-year-old Rosalind reportedly said to her, "I *know* Daddy likes *me*, and would like to be with me. It's *you* he doesn't seem to like."

Agatha eventually accepted that her marriage was over. The Matrimonial Causes Act of 1923 made it possible for a woman to gain a divorce on the grounds of her spouse's adultery; Archie would just need to admit to his affair with Nancy Neele. Rather than involve Nancy in the divorce, however, Archie convinced Agatha to agree to what was called a "Brighton Quickie." He would manufacture evidence of his adultery with "a woman unknown," and Agatha wouldn't mention Nancy.

On April 20, 1928, Agatha testified about the "woman unknown" under oath. By most accounts, the judge didn't believe the lies Mr. and Mrs. Christie told under oath, but he granted the divorce anyway. The dissolution of the Christies' marriage was finalized on October 29, 1928. Archie and Nancy married one week later. They had one child, a son, and remained together until Nancy's death from cancer in 1958.

THE MORE YOU KNOW

According to the UK Parliament website, divorce before 1914 was rare; there was just one divorce for every 450 marriages. World War I, with its multiple disruptions of family life, led to divorce law reforms. The Matrimonial Causes Act of 1923 enabled either partner to petition for divorce due to spousal adultery. A further act in 1937 offered additional grounds for divorce: cruelty, desertion, and incurable insanity.

Back to Work

Agatha was now a single mother who needed to make a living. Since Clara's death, Christie had felt no desire to write, but she had to honor her contract with Collins. The year before the divorce was finalized, Campbell Christie had suggested she collect the last twelve Poirot short stories she had published for *The Sketch* and rework them into an episodic novel. The result was *The Big Four*, her seventh novel. Published in January 1927, it generated poor reviews. "Those who have come to expect subtlety as well as sensation in Mrs. Christie's writings will be disappointed," wrote the *Daily Mail*. Yet the book sold a record 8,500 copies (likely due to the sensational coverage of her disappearance, scholars suggest).

Now, Christie was back to writing. In February 1928, she finished another novel, *The Mystery of the Blue Train*, while on vacation with Rosalind and Carlo in the Canary Islands. "Easily the worst book I have ever written," Christie would later say of the novel. It was published in March 1928 and sold seven thousand copies. Critics complained about the slowness of the opening and the withholding of crucial information until too late to guess the solution, but they also commended Christie for her characterization of heroine

Katherine Grey, her clever misdirections, and the luxury of the setting. Agatha did not enjoy writing the novel but later reflected, "That was the moment when I changed from an amateur to a professional. I assumed the burden of a profession, which is to write even when you don't want to. . . . I have always hated *The Mystery of the Blue Train*, but I got it written, and sent off to publishers."

Sometime in the fall of 1928, Christie also drafted *The Seven Dials Mystery*, a sequel to *Chimneys*, and it was published in 1929. By her own account, she had enjoyed writing *Chimneys* because, as a thriller, it required "less plotting and planning" than a detective novel. It also gave her the chance to write in a more lighthearted vein than in her Poirot novels; reviewers of both *Chimneys* and *Dials* noted what scholar Charles Osborne calls an "air of Wodehousian inconsequentiality and charm" in these two books.

LITERARY CONNECTIONS

P.G. Wodehouse was a prolific writer of the twentieth century, with over ninety books, more than two hundred short stories, and forty plays to his credit. He is best known for his Jeeves and Wooster series, which charts the adventures of an upper-class gentleman and his valet. Beyond *The Secret of Chimneys* and *The Seven Dials Mystery,* scholars note traces of Wode-house's signature charm in Christie's Tommy and Tuppence series and her Mr. Quin stories. (More on these later.)

Adapting Poirot

With Agatha back to work and going through a divorce, her novel *The Murder of Roger Ackroyd* was adapted for the stage. On May 15, 1928, just weeks after the Christies had gone to divorce court, *Alibi* premiered at the Prince of Wales Theatre in the West End. Twenty-eight-year-old Charles Laughton, the current golden boy of London theater, played Poirot.

To Agatha, *Alibi* was a huge disappointment. The book's character Caroline Sheppard (a spinster who would inspire another recurring Christie detective, Miss Marple) was replaced in the play by a younger, prettier female character. Christie later wrote of this change: "I resented the removal of Caroline a good deal: I liked the part she played in village life: and I like the idea of village life reflected through the life of the doctor and his masterful sister." Christie also felt that Charles Laughton was too young and too overweight to play Poirot.

Her problems with *Alibi* ran deeper, however. In Christie's view, Hercule Poirot should never be cast in a play. According to her, Poirot's presence would overshadow other characters onstage as well as eclipse the plot. Christie also believed detective stories like hers weren't right for theatrical adaptations because they involved a lot of reasoning and little action. And as *Alibi*, with its confused revelation of Dr. Sheppard as the murderer, seemed to prove, she also assumed her elaborate plot twists couldn't be staged (critics and audiences alike seemed to enjoy everything about *Alibi* except the final revelation).

After seeing *Alibi*, Agatha decided that *she* would adapt one of her novels—one in which Poirot doesn't appear. She chose her fifth novel, *The Secret of Chimneys*, which features a workaday detective named Superintendent Battle. Christie wrote the play quickly, but it never made it to the stage because London producers wanted Poirot.

A year later, Christie wrote an original play, this one featuring the Belgian detective. *Black Coffee* was a country house mystery involving the murder of a scientist. It premiered at the Embassy Theatre on December 8, 1930 to glowing reviews—and launched Christie's career as a playwright. However, she never wrote another full-length play featuring Poirot, and she excluded him from all her future theatrical adaptations.

THE MORE YOU KNOW

Contrary to Christie's disapproval, it was Charles Laughton's performance as Poirot that garnered the greatest praise from critics reviewing *Alibi*. The *Daily Express* described his performance as "so subtle, and yet so dominating, that it gripped the house. At the end the shout 'Laughton! Laughton,' to which we're becoming accustomed, was heard on every hand."

From Black Coffee, Act I

RICHARD. "Yes. I'm sorry. Too bad dragging you down. Of course, your fee—I mean that will be alright."

POIROT. "I comprehend perfectly. But for the moment it is not money that interests me."

RICHARD. "What . . . ?"

POIROT. "What does interest me? Just a little point. It was your father who sent for me to come. Why is it not he who tells me to go?"

RICHARD. "Oh, of course. I'm sorry."

(He turns to SIR CLAUD.)

RICHARD. "Father, please tell Monsieur Poirot we have no need of his services."

(There is no answer.)

RICHARD. "Father!"

(He rushes over to SIR CLAUD, bends over him, then turns wildly.)

"Doctor!"

(AUNT CAROLINE rises and moves to SIR CLAUD's side. CARELLI follows and begins an examination. POIROT feels SIR CLAUD's pulse, then steps back and looks at the dead man. He speaks softly, as if to himself.)

POIROT. "Ye—es—I fear, I very much fear—"

BARBARA. "What do you fear?"

POIROT. "That SIR CLAUD has sent for me too late, Mademoiselle."

Christie Tricks

As a professional writer, Christie would settle into a preferred length of 50,000–60,000 words for each novel. She'd make use of almost everything in her life, from her travels and second husband's occupation to the details of her homes and meals, for her fiction. And she'd develop familiar devices and strategies that her readers would come to expect: "Christie Tricks," Lucy Worsley calls them. Readers can see these tricks at work as early as in her first detective novel, *The Mysterious Affair at Styles*. They continue throughout her career, right up to her last novel, *Postern of Fate*, published in 1973.

One trick is to hide a key object, like a murder weapon, in plain sight. Spoiler alert: In *Cards on the Table*, for example, the murder weapon turns out to be an ornamental dagger in a display case, visible to all the guests. Another trick is the secret couple, two lovers plotting a crime together who pretend to not know or to hate each other. Examples include Jacqueline de Bellefort and Simon Doyle in *Death on the Nile* and Ada Mason and Major Richard Knighton in *The Mystery of the Blue Train*.

A third trick is to set the crime in places familiar to the author. In *Dead Man's Folly*, Christie used her own boathouse as the scene of a murder. *Five Little Pigs* features her own gardens at Greenway as the location of the novel's crimes. Another trick is to populate her novels with mystery fans. Miss Marple, Caroline Sheppard in *The Murder of Roger Ackroyd*, and Colonel Bantry in *The Body in the Library*: These characters all devour mysteries. In *Library*, another character, Peter Carmody, says, "Do you like detective stories? I do. I read them all, and I've got autographs from Dorothy Sayers and Agatha Christie and Dickson Carr and H.C. Bailey."

A fifth trick is the omission of facts by someone readers trust. In *Endless Night*, the narrator withholds his identity and motivations, leading us to form a false sense of security and sympathy. In *Curtain*, the novel that ends the career, and life, of Hercule Poirot, the famous detective withholds the revelation of his actions from both Hastings and us until the very end of the story. Several Christie Tricks have become essential tips for would-be crime writers.

THE MORE YOU KNOW

For a full list of Christie Tricks, visit the website https://careerauthors.com/christie-tips-on-mystery-writing.

The Orient Express

By the fall of 1928, Rosalind was in school and Agatha had a new, different kind of novel (*Giant's Bread*) underway. It was then that she decided to travel to the West Indies for a vacation. However, two days before the trip, she met a couple who'd just returned from Baghdad. When Agatha learned from the couple that she could reach Baghdad by the Orient Express, she hastened to the travel agency Thomas Cook & Son and swapped her ticket.

The Orient Express, a train service connecting Eastern and Western Europe, was launched in 1883. Between 1926 and 1929, decorator René Prou and master glassmaker René Lalique created the train's new Pullman lounge cars featuring marquetry, molded glass, and leather and velvet seating. By the time Agatha was onboard, the Orient Express had become synonymous with luxury and opulence.

The passage took her from London to Paris to Lausanne to Milan and so on, ending in Beirut. From Beirut, she took a "rickety bus" (as Janet Morgan calls it) to Baghdad. Once in Baghdad, she traveled to the ancient city of Ur. At the time, Ur was well known due to archaeologist Leonard Woolley. Working in Baghdad since 1922, Woolley believed that the ruins of Ur held traces of the biblical Great Flood.

His excavation had thus far yielded many finds, including a gold dagger in a sheath of lapis lazuli and gold. Having read of Woolley's discoveries in *The Illustrated London News*, Agatha wanted to see the excavation for herself. And while most visitors were sent away from the site, Woolley's wife, Katharine (a huge fan of *The Murder of Roger Ackroyd*), arranged for the author to be allowed in.

Agatha was given not only a tour of the excavation but also an invitation to dine with the Woolleys. It marked the beginning of a friendship that would have a lasting impact on Agatha's life.

The More You Know

Katharine Woolley (née Menke) was an illustrator and archaeologist. She met Leonard Woolley in 1924 while working as a field assistant in Ur. In 1925, Leonard offered her an official position as an illustrator for the excavation. But the presence of a young single woman among unmarried men made trustees at the University of Pennsylvania (joint funders of the expedition) uncomfortable. Leonard eventually married Katharine two years later—with her condition that the marriage never be consummated.

A New House, More Writing, and a Notorious Murder Case

Agatha returned home from Baghdad at Christmastime and soon bought a new house in Chelsea. Here, she practiced cooking in her new kitchen, trying out Middle Eastern dishes like Circassian chicken and making impromptu breakfasts for unexpected visitors, according to Janet Morgan.

Nearing forty, Agatha was also making scads of money. The year before, her agent, Edmund Cork, had arranged for a new contract with Collins for her next six novels. The contract specified an advance of 750 pounds (roughly 40,000 pounds today) for each book and a royalty of 20 percent for the first eight thousand copies, and 25 percent for any book after that. With Dodd, Mead & Co., her American publisher, Cork arranged an advance of $2,500 (roughly $47,000 today) per book, with 15 percent royalties on the first 25,000 copies and 20 percent after that.

While enjoying the success of her previous works, Agatha continued writing steadily through 1929. She wrote *The Murder at the Vicarage*, *Giant's Bread*, and her first play, *Black Coffee*, while also working on several Mr. Quin stories. In addition, she published *The Seven Dials Mystery*, her ninth novel, and a collection of stories, *Partners in Crime*.

1929 was also the year of the highly publicized Croydon case. Beginning in April 1928, three members of a middle-class family living in Croydon were fatally poisoned with arsenic over the course of a year. The case was never solved, though the press blamed Grace Duff, wife of one of the victims.

In 1929, Christie wrote an article on the murders, "The Tragic Family of Croydon," at the request of the *Sunday Chronicle*. While she was unable to solve the crime, she would later draw on its elements in her fiction, including the case's three related but baffling killings. In *Three Act Tragedy* (1934), for example, Poirot says of the three, apparently disconnected murders under investigation, "Understand the first murder, and you will understand them all"—an echo of Christie's argument about the Croydon family poisonings: "There seems no conceivable way in which the death of these three persons would benefit any other one person, yet the similarity of the means shows that it must be one person. . . ."

LITERARY CONNECTIONS

Among the Croydon elements that inspired Christie were anonymous letters. Surviving members of the Croydon family were barraged by poison-pen letters from unknown senders. Years later in *The Moving Finger* (1942), Agatha would depict the effects on a village and its residents after each one receives a letter attacking their character.

A Faithful Dog

Sometime in 1928, after her divorce, Agatha took stock of her relationships, organizing each person into two categories she named the Order of the Faithful Dogs and the Order of the Rats. The Faithful Dogs were those who'd been loyal and supportive during the difficult years of her divorce—Madge and James Watts; Campbell Christie; her friend, Nan Watts; Edmund Cork; and her assistant, Charlotte Fisher.

Charlotte Fisher, nicknamed "Carlo" by Rosalind and Agatha, was tall and thin. By most accounts, her appearance was intimidating, but she also had a "nice-looking twinkle," according to Agatha. Carlo had been Christie's assistant since 1924, when she answered the writer's advertisement for someone to supervise Rosalind and, while Rosalind attended school, work as a secretary. According to rare book dealer Peter Harrington, Agatha had added "Scottish preferred" to the advertisement, believing those of Scottish descent to be natural disciplinarians. Carlo Fisher's parents were both Scottish.

Born five years before Christie, Carlo was the daughter of an Edinburgh chaplain and eventually became a nanny and governess. Unmarried throughout her life, she worked for a variety of employers before Christie hired her.

Part of Carlo's job included living with Christie after Archie and Agatha got divorced. She would continue to reside with her boss in a succession of houses. A kind of second mother to Rosalind, Carlo reportedly gave Agatha's daughter more attention than Agatha did. Carlo also took on a wide range of secretarial duties as Christie's fame grew. As Rosalind later recalled, "She was much more than a secretary and I doubt if my mother could have managed without her." Between 1928 and 1929, as Agatha emerged from the darkness of the past few years, Carlo took dictation for parts of her novels, answered Agatha's correspondence, looked after her boss's new home in Chelsea when Agatha traveled, and visited Rosalind at school.

LITERARY CONNECTIONS

One of the most famous secretaries in literary history is Miss Felicity Lemon, Hercule Poirot's smart and efficient assistant, who appears in four novels and four short stories. Given Agatha's tendency to develop her fictional characters by incorporating personality traits from people she knew, some scholars believe Miss Lemon was based on Carlo Fisher.

Prodigal Brother

While Agatha was enjoying a productive year, her brother, Monty, was living out his last months in Marseilles. The past ten or so years had been difficult for him; while serving as a captain in East Africa during World War I, he had been wounded in the arm and, because of improper medical treatment, caught an infection in 1918 that severely compromised his health. He returned home ill.

Monty spent the next few years roaming through the Ashfield house in the middle of the night and waking the servants at 4 a.m. to cook dinner for him. He would also sit at his bedroom window and, when visitors walked up the drive, shoot his revolver at them. (Years later, Agatha would use this bit of family history to portray the murder victim in the play *The Unexpected Guest* [1958], who sends "shots to right and left of" a little old lady going down a drive.)

In 1923, Agatha and Madge pooled their resources and bought a cottage in Dartmoor for their brother to live in, hiring a woman named Mrs. Taylor to take care of him. A sixty-five-year-old widow, Mrs. Taylor reportedly doted on Monty. The Dartmoor cottage, however, was damp and remote, so a few years later, the sisters arranged for Monty and Mrs. Taylor to live in a small pensione in the French countryside.

While en route to France, Mrs. Taylor caught pneumonia and died. Monty convinced a young nurse named Charlotte, working at the local hospital, to take care of him in Mrs. Taylor's stead, supporting Agatha's later observation that "throughout his life [Monty] was surrounded by people anxious to save him worry or bother." According to Agatha, Charlotte "kept control of the purse strings—whilst tactfully listening to Monty's grandiose plans for living on a large yacht." But his health had been deteriorating steadily. He'd also become addicted to opiates ever since his wartime injury, and he drank and smoked frequently. In September 1929, he died of a stroke after finishing a cocktail at a seaside café. He was forty-nine years old.

Judging from her autobiography, Agatha seems to have felt some relief at Monty's death. By all accounts, he had caused her family much anxiety and frustration while he was alive. But she would also remember his charm and gift for living: "I think, being Monty, he enjoyed himself to the end."

LITERARY CONNECTIONS

Agatha would portray her brother, Monty, in her fiction as various charming rogues who get by on their good looks and knack for deception. Among them are James Pearson in *The Sittaford Mystery* (1931), Simon Doyle in *Death on the Nile* (1937), and Michael Rogers in *Endless Night* (1967). Critic Jake Kerridge suggests that Monty was also the basis for Agatha's portrayal of the charming, wildly unpredictable Jacko Argyle in *Ordeal by Innocence* (1958).

Introducing Miss Marple

The year after Monty's passing, a new Christie character made her debut: Miss Marple. Introduced in Christie's tenth novel, *The Murder at the Vicarage*, Miss Marple is first described as "the worst cat in the village."

Just as Christie employed the stereotype of the comic foreigner for Poirot, she used the convention of the nosy, elderly woman spying on her neighbors to create Miss Marple. Like Poirot, whom the police and criminals continually underestimate, Miss Marple uses her status as an elderly spinster to camouflage her detective activities. "Old ladies are supposed to be inquisitive," she tells the young Gwenda Halliday in *Sleeping Murder* (1976).

Unlike Poirot, however, whose cases often take place in foreign countries, Miss Marple solves crimes close to home, in the fictional village of St. Mary Mead. Marple is also cynical compared to Poirot. "I'm afraid that observing human nature for as long as I have done," she says in *The Murder at the Vicarage*, "one gets not to expect very much from it."

Scholars and fans of Christie believe that it is through Miss Marple that the author highlights the ways in which women think. In Marple's questions and observations, Christie brings to light the key domestic details her male counterparts don't catch. (In *The Murder at the Vicarage*, for example, she observes that Mrs. Protheroe's dress is too formfitting to conceal a gun.) Marple also draws parallels between the crime she currently studies and small, domestic incidents that have happened in St. Mary Mead.

After *Vicarage*, another twelve years would go by before Christie published more novels featuring Marple (*The Body in the Library* and *The Moving Finger*, both in 1942), and eight more years would pass before she would publish a third (*A Murder Is Announced*, 1950). After that, it was full steam ahead, with Marple rivaling Poirot in the number of novels featuring each. A sharp-witted woman who combats ageism and solves crimes, Miss Marple is often seen by fans of Christie as an alter ego for the aging author. Just as Miss Marple hides her detection through "old lady" habits and occupations, for example, Christie concealed her own career ambitions by posing as an ordinary, conventional woman.

THE MORE YOU KNOW

Miss Marple sheds light on a social issue of the early twentieth century: the "surplus woman." Coined sometime in the mid-nineteenth century, the term refers to a then-perceived surplus of unmarried women in Britain caused by fatalities in war and such social changes as more education for women. Older single women were viewed as a "special problem," given their inability to procreate.

From The Body in the Library, Chapter 1

Mrs. Bantry's voice came breathless and agitated over the wires.

"The most awful thing has happened."

"Oh, my dear."

"We've just found a body in the library."

For a moment, Miss Marple thought her friend had gone mad.

"You've found a *what*?"

"I know. One doesn't believe it, does one? I mean, I thought they only happened in books. I had to argue with Arthur for hours this morning before he'd even go down and see."

Miss Marple tried to collect herself. She demanded breathlessly: "But whose body is it?"

"It's a blonde."

"A what?"

"A beautiful blonde—like books again. None of us have ever seen her before. She's just lying there in the library, dead. That's why you've got to come up at once."

"You want me to come up?"

"Yes, I'm sending the car down for you."

Miss Marple said doubtfully: "Of course, dear, if you think I can be of any comfort to you—"

"Oh, I don't want comfort. But you're so good at bodies."

"No Feminine Intuition, Mumbo Jumbo, or Jiggery-Pokery"

It started in the late 1920s with a few dinners at the house of Anthony Berkeley, a fellow crime writer. Berkeley's charm was legendary—seen as more remarkable for how he was ailing and asthmatic (during World War I, he'd been exposed to mustard gas). But more legendary still was his campaign to elevate the detective genre. Guests at Berkeley's dinners included Christie, Dorothy L. Sayers, and G.K. Chesterton. By 1930, the guest list had expanded to twenty-eight crime writers who called their group the "Detection Club." The club was formed for two purposes: to aid one another with their writing and to promote detective fiction as a serious genre with its own specific standards and practices. Mainly, the club had dinners. In full evening attire, members would meet once a month at the Café Royal in London to discuss crime matters. Sometimes, guests, such as London's chief of forensics, were invited to give lectures.

Agatha remained a club member until her death. And in 1957, when Sayers, who had become the club's third president, unexpectedly died, Christie took over. Christie's one condition: that she share the position with Lord Gorell so she wouldn't have to make speeches.

The Detection Club's initiation rituals are legendary. Crime writer Lucy Beatrice Malleson described her initiation in the early 1930s: Dorothy L. Sayers, wearing black robes, led her down a hall lit with lamps. At Sayers's instruction, Malleson put her hand over a skull (placed on a velvet cushion), while the club's president, G.K. Chesterton, dressed in a bright red cape, intoned the club's commandments. Malleson then solemnly swore that she would make no use whatsoever of "Divine Revelation, Feminine Intuition, Mumbo Jumbo, Jiggery-Pokery, Coincidence, or Act of God," that she would "conceal no vital clues from the reader," and that she would "honour the King's English." According to club rules, should she fail to uphold these vows, a curse would befall her: "May other writers anticipate your plots, may total strangers sue you for libel, may your pages swarm with misprints, and your sales continually diminish!"

LITERARY CONNECTIONS

Six Detection Club members, including Christie, Dorothy L. Sayers, and Anthony Berkeley, collaborated on a thriller series called *Behind the Screen* for the BBC in 1930. A year later, they did another series called *The Scoop*. Members of the club also cowrote the novels *The Floating Admiral* (1931), *Ask a Policeman* (1933), and *The Sinking Admiral* (2016); and a cluster of short story anthologies including *Six Against the Yard* (1936) and *The Anatomy of Murder* (1936).

"By Some Curious Effect"

In 1930, Agatha published a short story collection that she later called "my favourite." The collection didn't include Poirot or Miss Marple. Rather, its protagonist is a supernatural, Eros-like figure named Harley Quin, who solves mysteries that mortals can't, and ensures the happiness of young lovers.

One reason these stories appealed to Agatha was because they were hers to write how and when she wanted to. Magazines had offered Agatha money to serialize the stories, but she turned them all down: "I didn't want to do a series of Mr. Quin: I only wanted to do one when I felt like it." Ultimately she wrote one Quin story every three or four months and published them in a wide range of American and British magazines.

In 1930, Collins published twelve Quin stories under the title *The Mysterious Mr. Quin*. In her autobiography, she described the Quin collection as her "favorite" of all her story collections (there are fourteen collections total). It is the only book of Christie's to be dedicated to its protagonist. The first story of the collection is "The Coming of Mr. Quin," originally published in *The Grand Magazine* in March 1924. In this story, Agatha introduced her protagonist by describing how he "appeared by some curious effect of the stained glass above the door, to be dressed in every colour of the rainbow." Christie would use this description in every Quin story to follow, linking her creation with the traditional harlequin figure dressed in a checkered costume.

Like his harlequin prototype, Quin subverts authority (whether the police or the laws of nature) and maintains a carefree, cheerful attitude in whatever situation he faces, including murder. Quin has an assistant named Mr. Satterthwaite, whom Christie portrays as "a little bent, dried-up man with a peering face oddly elflike, and an intense and inordinate interest in other people's lives." Satterthwaite describes himself as "an observer of life." Together, Quin and Satterthwaite clear up a ten-year-old murder case, free a young man from wrongful imprisonment, and prove that a presumably innocent wife is a criminal plotting to steal her husband's fortune.

THE MORE YOU KNOW

"The Coming of Mr. Quin" was made into a British film called *The Passing of Mr. Quinn* ("n" added) in 1928, a year before a German adaptation of *The Secret Adversary* (titled *Die Abenteurer G.m.b.H.*) appeared. *The Passing of Mr. Quinn* departs radically from the story by making Quin a murderer. In 1929, a novelization of the same title, written by G. Roy McRae, was published by the London Book Company.

Alias, Mary Westmacott

Stepping even further from Poirot and Marple in 1930, Agatha Christie invented a pseudonym for herself and wrote a book much different from her detective fiction. Published under the name Mary Westmacott, the book was *Giant's Bread*. It is here, biographer Charles Osborne speculates, that Christie "found that she was not only a creator of brilliant puzzles but a real novelist."

Christie would publish five more titles under this pseudonym: *Unfinished Portrait* (1934), *Absent in the Spring* (1944), *The Rose and the Yew Tree* (1948), *A Daughter's a Daughter* (1952), and *The Burden* (1956). As she would explain in her autobiography, she wrote them as a break from her day job.

In the Westmacott novels, Christie writes not about the mystery of murder but about the mystery of the human heart. As scholar Merja Makinen argues, the theme running through all six Westmacott novels is a lesson Agatha likely learned from the events of 1926: namely, "Real love is about leaving the other alone . . . because everyone is essentially unknowable." Christie had always woven elements from her own life into her fiction. But in these six novels, she writes about her life in much more depth. Her heroines are engaged in plots that involve adultery, divorce, suicide attempts, and mother-daughter relationships—all key themes of Christie's own life.

Written in three days, Agatha's third Westmacott novel, *Absent in the Spring,* turned out to be her favorite book among all her novels. She described it as "the one book that has satisfied me completely . . . the book that I had always wanted to write."

Then, in 1949, Agatha would be outed. The Atticus column in *The Sunday Times* revealed that Mary Westmacott and Agatha Christie were one and the same. Although she wrote two more Westmacott novels (*A Daughter's a Daughter* and *The Burden*) after this public revelation, critics agree that these latter books don't measure up to the first three. "It's really all washed up," she wrote to her agent, Edmund Cork, referring to her pseudonym and the revelatory, personal books it allowed her to write. Once again, Agatha had been exposed by the press.

THE MORE YOU KNOW

Published in *The Sunday Times,* the Atticus column is a weekly society and gossip column that started in the 1930s. Its columnist operates under the pseudonym Atticus. In 1949, Atticus was the journalist and food writer Cyril Ray. Ian Fleming, the literary creator of James Bond, served as Atticus from 1953 to 1956.

(Unfinished) Portrait of an Artist

One novel in the Westmacott series, *Unfinished Portrait,* reads very closely to Agatha's life story. Christie scholar Charles Osborne claims that the novel, published in 1934, "is much more overtly and directly autobiographical than the others [Westmacott novels]." Christie's second husband, Max Mallowan, agreed, writing in his memoir that "in Celia [the protagonist] we have more nearly than anywhere else a portrait of Agatha."

In *Unfinished Portrait,* Larraby, a successful portrait painter, tells the story of his relationship with Celia, a woman whom he first encounters just as she is about to drown herself in the sea. After the incident, Larraby accompanies her back to her hotel and spends the night in her room as she recounts the events of her life to him. Celia tells Larraby about meeting her husband, Dermot, at a regimental ball in York and how Dermot swept her off her feet and away from her fiancé. Dermot then grew indifferent toward his wife, eventually asking for a divorce.

Celia also tells Larraby about her youth—how she was a shy and imaginative child who shared a psychic bond with her mother and adored her formidable grandmother. Occasionally, she was haunted by nightmares of a strange figure who suddenly appeared out of nowhere, just as in Agatha's dreams of the Gunman. As a young woman, Celia studied music in Paris, hoping to become a professional singer (as Agatha did) until she decided she was too shy. Celia too had a debutante season in Egypt, where she attracted many admirers.

Like her creator, Celia is also a writer. She tells Larraby early in the novel that she found it impossible to write after her marriage ended. The novel's ending, however, suggests that Celia is on the way to becoming a more serious writer because of this difficult experience, just as Agatha had.

THE MORE YOU KNOW

In its December 9, 1934, review, *The New York Times* reported that the structure of *Unfinished Portrait,* with Celia telling Larraby her life story, "seems artificial and unnecessary at first, but is effectively used in the ending." The reviewer also wrote, "As a study of a shy, emotional nature, verging on the pathological, *Unfinished Portrait* is moderately well done. It is worth reading for its sympathetic—and sometimes very amusing—account of Celia's childhood."

From Unfinished Portrait, Chapter 7

"Dermot, is anything the matter?"

"What should be the matter?"

. . .

This wasn't Dermot—upright, handsome, laughing Dermot. . . . This was a furtive, shrinking person. . . . He looked—almost—like a criminal.

She said suddenly, "Dermot, there isn't anything—with money—I mean, you haven't done anything—?"

. . .

"There is something . . . I expect you can guess."

. . .

She said: "Tell me."

. . .

Dermot stood up. His voice sounded strange and stiff.

"It's—well, it's Marjorie Connell. I've seen a lot of her, I'm very fond of her."

. . .

"I don't understand. You just want to leave *us*?"

"Because I can't be any good to you. I should simply be foul."

"But we've been so happy—so happy."

Dermot said impatiently:

"Yes, of course we have—in the past. But we've been married eleven years. After eleven years one needs a change."

The Young Assistant

Agatha returned to Ur in March of 1930, just one month before *Giant's Bread* was published. There, she met Max Mallowan, Leonard Woolley's twenty-six-year-old assistant, who had been absent during her first visit due to appendicitis. Six months later, Max and Agatha would be married. Short and quiet, Max was described by Agatha as a "grave-looking" academic type, whose serious air initially intimidated her. But, as she later recalled, there was a calm assurance in Max Mallowan that soon attracted her to him.

One of Max's duties as Woolley's assistant was to show the excavation site at Ur to distinguished visitors. Katharine Woolley arranged for him to escort Agatha on a tour of local sights as the two of them made their way to Baghdad, where the excavation party was planning to reunite before journeying back to England. According to Lucy Worsley, a "kind of friendly intimacy" developed between the two. During the tour, they swam in a lake together in their undergarments, and each night, he'd escort her to an outhouse while they laughed about the awkwardness of the situation.

A few weeks later, on a train ride to Greece with the Woolleys and Max, Agatha received telegrams from Madge, informing her that Rosalind had pneumonia and was seriously ill. Agatha tried to find a faster way home but ended up spraining her ankle. Max took care of everything, accompanying her on the four-day train ride to Paris. There, they met his mother, a French woman named Marguerite, who lent Agatha money for her passage to England. By the time Agatha arrived home, Rosalind had recovered.

THE MORE YOU KNOW

In 1930, contracting pneumonia could be deadly. It wasn't until the mid-1940s that mass production of penicillin became widely available, though the first antibacterial agents, such as sulfapyridine, were developed in the 1930s. In 1930, pneumonia and influenza were the second leading cause of death in the UK and the US.

Nothing in the World

By her own account, Agatha didn't consider Max Mallowan to be marriage material. In her view, he was a friend. Fourteen years younger than she was, he was the same age as her nephew, James (called "Jack"), Madge's son. "It never occurred to me that Max and I would or ever could be on those terms. We were *friends*," she later wrote.

Regardless, a few months after they parted ways in Paris, they met up in London, where Max was working at the British Museum. Agatha invited him to come down to Ashfield. In his memoir, Max later recounted observing the same adaptability he had seen in Christie in Baghdad. Just as she had adapted to bugs and outhouses in Iraq, she adapted to the demands of a household and eleven-year-old daughter. As he would later write, it was at this time that he decided Agatha Christie would make a great wife, especially for a man like him, whose work involved a thousand inconveniences and annoyances.

During his stay at Ashfield, Max came into Agatha's bedroom one night on the pretense of returning a book he had borrowed. Instead, he proposed marriage. According to Agatha, she was shocked and listed the obstacles she saw—age difference, religious difference (he was Catholic; she was Anglican), his work, her work—telling him she'd think about it. When he left the next morning, he said, "I think you *will* marry me, you know."

Christie's family members, namely her brother-in-law, James Watts, and sister, Madge, objected to the idea of the marriage. Madge claimed that Agatha was making a "foolish" mistake in marrying Max. Rosalind, the "home oracle," as Agatha called her, however, liked the idea, citing that Max played tennis and sailed and that Peter, the family dog, seemed to like him. In the end, Agatha decided that "nothing in the world would be as delightful as being married to him."

Max and Agatha were married privately in September 1930, in Edinburgh. From there, they journeyed to Greece for a honeymoon that Agatha would describe as "unconventional." They walked in the groves of Olympia and went skinny-dipping in the sea at Dubrovnik, and also took long rides on buses infested with fleas and went on a fourteen-hour mule trek up and down ravines.

LITERARY CONNECTIONS

Soon after Max and Agatha's honeymoon, Max left for a five-month dig that Katharine Woolley declared Agatha could not attend. And so, the newlyweds were forced to be apart for the next five months. But Agatha got her revenge, as Christie biographers point out; in *Murder in Mesopotamia* (1936), she would kill off an archaeologist's wife who closely resembles Katharine Woolley.

From Death in the Clouds, Chapter 13

"You seem to think a lot about women and their looks," said Jane.

"Naturally. It is the most interesting subject possible. That seems strange to you because you are English. An Englishman thinks first of his work—his job, he calls it—and then of his sport, and last—a good way last—of his wife. Yes, yes, it is really so. Why, imagine, in a little hotel in Syria was an Englishman whose wife had been taken ill. He himself had to be somewhere in Iraq by a certain date. *Eh bien*, would you believe it, he left his wife and went on so as to be on duty in time. And both he and his wife thought that quite natural; they thought him noble, unselfish. But the doctor, who was not English, thought him a barbarian. A wife, a human being—that should come first. To do one's job—that is something much less important."

A Radio Adaptation

In April 1930, roughly one month after Agatha met Max Mallowan, she received a letter from Hilda Matheson, the BBC's first Director of Talks, inviting her to "join in a mystery serial." Christie was asked to write an installment of roughly 1,800 words that would be read, by her, alongside those of other "leading detective story-writers," including Ronald Knox, Dorothy L. Sayers, and E.C. Bentley, founders of the Detection Club.

The serial was called *Behind the Screen* and aired weekly on the BBC between June 14 and July 19, 1930. Christie's installment, "Something Is Missing," aired on June 21, 1930. It's a mystery set on a country estate, where a corpse is discovered behind a Chinese screen. The experience of producing it turned out to be exhilarating *and* irksome to Agatha, who, according to scholar Vike Martina Plock, enjoyed writing the fast-paced dialogue required of radio but disliked the BBC's heavy-handed edits and, it seemed, collaborative writing in general.

The BBC then commissioned a second serial, *The Scoop*, this one broadcast in twelve weekly installments. Set in a newspaper office where the body of a reporter is found, *The Scoop* aired weekly between January 10 and April 4, 1931.

Christie may have been reluctant to write collaboratively for the radio, but she jumped at the chance to adapt her own novels for a listening audience. In the 1930s, radio had evolved into a domestic mass medium. Prioritizing dialogue and minimizing description, it was ideal for conveying Christie's mysteries.

In 1934, Christie would write a radio play for the BBC called *Miss Marple Tells a Story*, in which the spinster sleuth helps save a friend of her solicitor's from the charge of having murdered his wife. According to Vike Martina Plock, the play was considered a "great success" at the BBC—and Miss Marple a "natural" for radio.

Meanwhile, other celebrities adapted Christie for the medium. Orson Welles did a live radio drama series of *The Murder of Roger Ackroyd*, scripted by Herman Mankiewicz, the Oscar-winning screenwriter of *Citizen Kane*, for *The Campbell Playhouse*. In it, Welles, who had a reputation for monopolizing roles, played Poirot, as well as the villain, Dr. Sheppard!

THE MORE YOU KNOW

In recent years, the BBC has produced a new string of Christie adaptations for the radio. All these adaptations are either of Miss Marple stories or of lesser-known works by Christie, such as her Westmacott novel *Giant's Bread* and her unpublished play, *The Lie*, about marital infidelity.

Heart Specialist, Parker Pyne

"You must remember I am not a detective. I am, if you like to put it that way, a heart specialist." These are the words of J. Parker Pyne, a retired civil servant who, after thirty-five years of statistical work in a government office, begins a new career. He engages a secretary (a young woman named Miss Felicity Lemon), sets up shop in a small London office, and runs an ad in *The Times*: "ARE YOU HAPPY? IF NOT, CONSULT MR. PARKER PYNE, 17 Richmond Street."

Christie created the character Parker Pyne in 1932 for a short story called "The Coming of Mr. Pyne," in which he establishes his peculiar business. Over the next two years, Pyne appeared in eleven more stories scattered in magazines like *Cosmopolitan* and *The Strand*. Collins published these stories in 1934 as a collection under the title *Parker Pyne Investigates*.

As a self-described "specialist of the heart," Pyne in his adventures confronts problems like stale marriages, infidelity, betrayal, and middle-aged loneliness: problems that had impacted the author's own life several years before. A statistician, Pyne theorizes that there are five types of unhappiness: "discontent with oneself," boredom, love troubles (romantic heartbreak, difficulty finding a romantic interest), domestic troubles (family tension, spousal discord), and misfortune (accidents, bad luck). Once the cause of the affliction is known, a cure should be possible. His first step is to categorize his client's unhappiness and then, consulting his files of previous cases, arrange a remedy.

So, in "The Case of the Middle-Aged Wife," when a woman visits Pyne complaining of her husband's affair with his young secretary, he knows what to do. First, he sends the wife to a salon and dress shop for a makeover. When she emerges with a new look, he introduces her to a young man (an actor hired by Pyne), who escorts her to the nightclubs where her husband has been conducting his illicit liaison. Just as Pyne planned, the husband sees his made-over wife with her young escort, and his interest is rekindled. The wife goes home happy, and Pyne solves another case of the heart.

THE MORE YOU KNOW

In 1935, Agatha would bring Felicity Lemon back, as Poirot's secretary in the short story "How Does Your Garden Grow?" Lemon wouldn't appear again until the later Poirot novels: *Hickory Dickory Dock* (1955), *Dead Man's Folly* (1956), *Third Girl* (1966), and *Elephants Can Remember* (1972). Along with Miss Marple and Ariadne Oliver, Miss Lemon became a recurring female character in Christie's later fiction.

"A Strong Dash of Myself"

Parker Pyne's cases of the heart led to another recurring character: Ariadne Oliver. Described as impulsive, frank, and mocking, with defiant hair and extravagant costumes, Oliver first appeared in the Pyne story "The Case of the Discontented Soldier" (1932). Four years later, Oliver emerged as a full-fledged character in *Cards on the Table* (1936). She would also appear in *Mrs. McGinty's Dead* (1952), *Dead Man's Folly* (1956), *Third Girl* (1966), *Hallowe'en Party* (1969), and *Elephants Can Remember* (1972).

Although Agatha always denied drawing her characters from her personal life, she did say that Oliver had "a strong dash of myself." Like her creator, Oliver is a bestselling crime writer. And just as Christie had an imaginary detective (Poirot) she openly disliked, so does Oliver. Of this detective, named Sven Hjerson, Oliver says, "How do I know why I ever thought of the revolting man? I must have been mad!"

Oliver is portrayed as "stout," with Christie's partiality for apples and expensive motor cars. Middle-aged and unmarried, she enjoys sleuthing, playing the role of intuitive amateur detective to Poirot's rational, methodical detection. Often criticizing men as incompetent or brutish, she is always on the watch for women she can help through her investigative interventions. Her recurring line is that a woman should be running Scotland Yard.

Biographers and avid fans of Christie note that as a humorous character, Oliver offers little challenge to Poirot or Miss Marple when it comes to sleuthing. However, as a writer, Oliver reveals a great deal about Christie's thoughts on the profession. She complains about being constantly pressured by publishers for a new book; required to attend book signings and events in her honor; and watch incompetent playwrights, like Robin Upward in *Mrs. McGinty's Dead*, adapt her characters.

Christie scholar J.C. Bernthal claims that Oliver "begins as a parody of stereotypes . . . and evolves into a strategic self-portrait." While he doesn't elaborate, others say that Christie's "strategy" was to give her public a bit of what they wanted: Christie herself, but at an ironic distance.

THE MORE YOU KNOW

In the TV series *Agatha Christie's Poirot*, Ariadne Oliver appears in series ten through thirteen, which ran from 2005 to 2013. She is played by actress Zoë Wanamaker, a Royal Shakespeare Company actress whose TV credits also include *Doctor Who* and *Killing Eve*. Wanamaker received glowing reviews for her performance. Julia McKenzie played Oliver in several BBC radio adaptations during the 2000s. And Jean Stapleton (of *All in the Family* fame), played Oliver in the 1986 adaptation of *Dead Man's Folly*.

From Mrs. McGinty's Dead, Chapter 10

"A book of mine is being dramatized—by Robin Upward. We're supposed to sort of get together over it."

"My felicitations, madame."

"It's not like that at all," said Mrs. Oliver. "So far it's pure *agony*. Why I ever let myself in for it I don't know. My books bring me in quite enough money—that is to say the bloodsuckers take most of it, and if I made more, they'd take more, so I don't overstrain myself. But you've no idea of the agony of having your characters taken and made to say things that they never would have said, and do things that they never would have done. And if you protest, all they say is that it's 'good theatre.' That's all Robin Upward thinks of. Everyone says he's very clever. If he's so clever I don't see why he doesn't write a play of his own and leave my poor unfortunate Finn alone. He's not even a Finn any longer. He's become a member of the Norwegian Resistance Movement."

She ran her hands through her hair. "What have I done with my hat?"

Poirot looked into the car.

"I think, madame, that you must have been sitting on it."

"Tell Mummy She Is Really a Pig!"

Christie biographers suggest that the relationship between Agatha and her daughter, Rosalind, was a strained one. By all accounts, Rosalind missed Archie terribly in the months after her parents' separation and divorce. Longing for their family life at Styles, she also resented having to live in a London apartment with her mother. In the fall of 1928, when she was nine, Rosalind was sent off to Caledonia, a preparatory school at Bexhill, then a three-hour train ride from London. Agatha recalls that Rosalind enjoyed it there. But as Christie biographers have speculated, Rosalind must have felt some hurt and resentment at being sent away from home so soon after her parents' divorce.

When Agatha started traveling annually to the Middle East in 1930, letters reveal that Rosalind often felt neglected. Her mother was gone for months at a time, writing her daughter sporadically and sending only brief notes when she did. "Would you mind telling me when you are coming home?" Rosalind asked in one letter to her mother. "You seem to tell Carlo and not me." Laura Thompson details that it was Agatha's assistant, Carlo, who filled in the gaps by sending Rosalind lots of cards at school and apprising her of Agatha's activities and plans. Biographers point to one letter by Rosalind, written in mock anger to Max, as barely concealing her real emotions:

"Before I forget, tell Mummy she is really a pig!! I have just had a letter from Carlo in which she says Mummy has let Ashfield until March. How could she! It makes me absolutely miserable. This will be the first time I haven't had my birthday there. I believe it is all your fault too with your archaeological conferences and things. I just hate you all but perhaps I shall get over it."

A solid student at Caledonia, Rosalind turned into a desultory one at her next school, Benenden. Her headmistress said in a report written in the summer of 1935, "I have felt throughout her time here that she has only achieved mediocrity. I am sorry that she is leaving us before being in a position to develop a sense of responsibility." Rosalind would continue to flounder in the coming years, while her mother had her most fruitful and happiest years yet.

LITERARY CONNECTIONS

In 1952, Agatha published *A Daughter's a Daughter,* her fifth Westmacott novel. It's the story of a teenage daughter's opposition to her middle-aged mother's plans to remarry. Originally, Agatha wrote it as a play in the 1930s, though it wasn't produced as such until July 9, 1956. Purportedly, Rosalind, who owned the rights to the story, refused to have it staged in the years between her mother's death in 1976 and her own passing in 2004 because she feared viewers would assume it was based on her relationship with Agatha.

Mrs. Mallowan

A photo from the 1950s shows Agatha and Max at an excavation site at Nimrud. He is taking measurements of a found object as she photographs it. It's an image of a married couple working together as a team, and based on her account as well as those of her biographers, it's also an accurate portrayal of their relationship. In her second husband, Agatha found a true companion. "Max and Agatha were a singularly loving and harmonious couple," scholar Gillian Gill observes. After Agatha died, a love letter Max had written her in 1930 was found folded up in her purse.

It was a traditional marriage in many ways. As a young woman, Agatha had been advised by her mother and grandmothers never to neglect her husband. When Archie declared that he was leaving her for Nancy Neele, Agatha recalled blaming herself, convinced that she hadn't paid enough attention to her husband's growing unhappiness. When she married Max, she resolved never to make that mistake again. So, Agatha accompanied her husband on his digs. She joined Max when he signed up with the Campbell Thompson party excavating Ninevah after Max's work at Ur ended in 1931. And she joined Max again a few years later, when he secured funding for three seasons to do his own archaeological dig in Chagar Bazar, Syria.

While at these sites, she continued to write books but mainly played the role of helpmate to her husband. "Agatha found camp life agreeable," Janet Morgan describes. According to Morgan, Christie liked its simplicity, the open air, and the sense of fraternity among the excavators. Still, she'd always been a woman who liked her comfort and luxury. At Chagar Bazar, a settlement mound near Nagar, she organized the supply of furniture and other provisions, scoured the countryside for fresh produce, and had Edmund Cork's office provide tinned and dried goods. The workmen "regarded her as a mother and a queen," in Morgan's words. Agatha would work with orange sticks and face cream to remove the dirt and dust from pottery during the digs. She also took hundreds of photos of objects found at the site, developing and classifying them herself. Then, when she'd had enough of the hot desert sun, the mosquito bites, and camp beds, she would return to her comfortable life at home, continuing to write her novels and pen love letters to Max.

LITERARY CONNECTIONS

In 1946, Christie published *Come, Tell Me Where You Live,* a "meandering chronicle . . . full of everyday doings and happenings," as she called it, of her adventures in Syria with her husband, Max. As Gillian Gill observes, the book allows the public a rare glimpse into Agatha's private life.

Plutocracy

Agatha loved houses: buying them, renovating them, and decorating them. During the 1930s, as she and Max settled into their married life, she bought eight of them. Her "plutocratic period," she called it.

One of these residences was Winterbrook, or "Max's house," purchased in 1934. Located on the River Thames in Wallingford, near Oxford, it was close to a main road but screened by holly bushes. At Winterbrook, Max had his own study, lined with bookshelves that carried archaeological journals and classics, including his favorite, *Histories* by Herodotus. The house also had a garden that stretched down to the Thames. Poet and historian A.L. Rowse, who stayed at Winterbrook often, described it as "a cosy, warm, hospitable" house with "all the comforts and amenities, the pretty china and good furniture that Agatha's prosperity has brought."

Agatha liked Winterbrook, but in 1938, she found the house of her dreams. Greenway, situated on the River Dart in Devon, would be her true home for the rest of her life. Originally built as a Tudor mansion around 1530, it had been destroyed in a fire and rebuilt in the late eighteenth century. Agatha would always describe it as a house out of her imagination.

Agatha bought Greenway and its 33 acres for 6,000 pounds, the equivalent of a very low 516,000 pounds today. She hired architect Guilford Bell to renovate the home. When it was finished, Greenway had five rooms on the first floor, including a master bedroom and a spacious bathroom paneled in mahogany. The upstairs had more bedrooms and a bed-sitting room for Rosalind; behind were the servant quarters and a massive kitchen. "Everything was high, deep, rightful. Everywhere was secrecy, enchantment, mystery. A glamorous house on the grand scale, yet relaxed and full of ease," as Thompson puts it.

None of the eight houses Agatha owned in the 1930s had a dedicated writing room for her. Dining tables, the marble washstand in a bedroom, side tables: These were her desks. The corner of any available room was her office. As Lucy Worsley explains, she wrote "on the edges of what she professed to think were the larger matters of life: shopping, eating, relaxing." This casual approach to writing would be a part of her public image throughout her career.

The More You Know

To raise the money to buy Greenway, Agatha sold Ashfield. Her childhood home had been overtaken by suburbia by this time, and a mental asylum had been built next door. When Agatha heard of its impending demolition in the early 1960s, she tried to buy it back, but it was too late.

From Death on the Nile, Chapter 7

"I wanted to make Wode Hall into my ideal of a country house, and I do think I've got it nice, don't you?"

"It's beautiful. Beautifully planned. Everything perfect. You're very clever, Linnet."

He paused a minute and went on:

"And you like Charltonbury, don't you? Of course it wants modernizing and all that—but you're so clever at that sort of thing. You enjoy it."

"Why, of course, Charltonbury's divine."

She spoke with ready enthusiasm, but inwardly she was conscious of a sudden chill. An alien note had sounded, disturbing her complete satisfaction with life.

She did not analyze the feeling at the moment, but later, when Windlesham had left her, she tried to probe the recesses of her mind.

Charltonbury—yes, that was it—she had resented the mention of Charltonbury. But why? Charltonbury was modestly famous. Windlesham's ancestors had held it since the time of Elizabeth. To be mistress of Charltonbury was a position unsurpassed in society. Windlesham was one of the most desirable parts in England.

Naturally, he wouldn't take Wode seriously. . . . It was not in any way to be compared with Charltonbury.

Ah, but Wode was hers! She had seen it, acquired it, rebuilt and re-dressed it, lavished money on it. It was her own possession, her kingdom.

Murder on the Orient Express

In early 1934, Christie published her most renowned novel. She dedicated it to Max, who first suggested the solution of the murder to her, and wrote it in six weeks while on a dig in Iraq. The novel is *Murder on the Orient Express,* in which twelve people, ranging from a Swedish missionary to an aged countess, are involved in the murder of a blackguard named Ratchett. Two main influences shaped the novel: the abduction and murder of Charles Lindbergh Jr., baby son of aviator Charles Lindbergh, in 1932, and the glamorous Orient Express, a perfect setting for the locked-room mystery in which Christie specialized.

While readers may think that crimes in Christie's fiction are pure invention, she based many of her novels on true-life cases. Her play *The Mousetrap* was inspired by the tale of Dennis O'Neill, who'd been killed by his foster parents. For the subplot of *Mrs. McGinty's Dead* (1952), she used the ghoulish case of Dr. Hawley Crippen, a medicine dispenser like Christie. In 1910, Crippen murdered his wife, buried her in their basement, and then moved his mistress into the house.

For *Orient,* Christie borrowed several elements from the Lindbergh case, which had occurred just two years prior. In both the case and the novel, for example, the kidnappers murdered the child despite the ransom being paid in full. Both also contain a suicide and a glamorous, high-profile couple. Christie's use of the posh Orient Express train was based on her actual travels aboard it. (After her first journey on the Orient in 1928, she traveled on the train several more times.)

One trip in particular gave her the circumstance for her novel's plot. In 1931, Christie was returning to England from Iraq when the train was stopped by a flood. "My darling, what a journey!" she wrote her husband a few days later. "Started out from Istanbul in a violent thunder storm. We went very slowly during the night and about 3 a.m. stopped altogether." As she recounts in this letter, the next two days brought a series of adventures: twelve hours stuck in a cold train, a mysterious man who kept trying to open the door between their compartments in the middle of the night, and an "American woman who never stopped talking." This woman would inspire Mrs. Hubbard, a key character in the *Orient*'s murder plot.

LITERARY CONNECTIONS

Murder on the Orient Express provided a new twist on what critics call the "Christie scenario": a murder, a detective, and a small group of people trapped together who slowly realize that one of them is the killer. Agatha would use this scenario repeatedly in novels like _The Sittaford Mystery_ (1931), _Cards on the Table_ (1936), and _And Then There Were None_ (1939).

Drama Queen

In her lifetime, Christie penned twenty-two full-length plays, according to theater historian Julius Green. One of them, *The Mousetrap*, still holds the honor of being the longest-running play of all time. Christie is also the only woman in history to have had three works—*The Mousetrap*, *Witness for the Prosecution*, and *Spider's Web*—run simultaneously in the West End, London's prestigious theater district.

Theater fascinated the young Christie, as it did all her family. "We were all lovers of the theatre in my family," she would write in her autobiography. Throughout the 1910s and 1920s, as Christie pressed on with her mystery novels, she also wrote multiple one-act and full-length plays before the 1930 premiere of *Black Coffee*, her first dramatic work to be produced.

One of these plays, written sometime between 1915 and 1920, was an adaptation of Arthur Reeve's detective novel *The Clutching Hand*. It's believed that Reeve's story appealed to Christie not only because of its focus on crime but also because of its depiction of a character type that would become a Christie trademark: the feisty young heroine who helps solve a case. Another Christie play that scholars take note of is *The Lie*, a "domestic drama" about marital infidelity and divorce. Its protagonist is Nan Gregg, a bored housewife whose husband spends more time with his golf clubs than with her. Scholars view this play with particular interest given the marital troubles that led up to Christie's disappearance in 1926.

Despite the opening of *Black Coffee* in 1930, the remainder of the decade was full of frustration for Christie as a playwright. Following *Black Coffee*, she wrote seven full-length plays encompassing a variety of styles and subjects. But viewers wanted to see Poirot, who was not featured in any of these plays. Only one of them, a psychological thriller titled *Love from a Stranger* (based on her story "Philomel Cottage") was performed, though it wasn't credited. It wouldn't be until 1943, when her most famous novel, *And Then There Were None*, was adapted for the stage that Agatha Christie would start to come into her own as a playwright. (More on this later.)

LITERARY CONNECTIONS

Love from a Stranger **focuses on Celia Harrington, whose life takes a dramatic turn when she wins a sweepstake. Enter Bruce Lovell, a seductive young man who happens to be a serial killer. Lovell is one of many young men in Christie's fiction and plays who turns out to be untrustworthy or worse. This play also explores a theme Christie would return to repeatedly: the choice between a placid existence and uncertain adventure.**

And Then There Were None

In November 1939, roughly two months after Britain declared war on Germany, Christie published *And Then There Were None*, which she later described as the most challenging of all her novels to write. She explained, "I had written the book . . . because it was so difficult to do that the idea had fascinated me. Ten people had to die without it becoming ridiculous or the murderer being obvious."

And Then There Were None appeared at the height of Christie's career, when she was publishing an average of two novels per year and experimenting with form. Along with *Murder on the Orient Express*, it continues to be the bestselling and most celebrated of all her mysteries. In fact, as of 2025, it's the bestselling crime novel of all time. And there are theories as to why this is so. "Well," says screenwriter Sarah Phelps, "You can see it as a game; it's a very, very clever plot." As with *The Murder of Roger Ackroyd*, it's nearly impossible to guess the perpetrator's identity. Moreover, all the classic Christie elements are here but to amplified effect: a remote house on an island the characters can't escape; a small group of suspects, each with a sordid secret; and a glamorous but unwelcoming setting.

And Then There Was None is also considered terrifying by many readers. Ten strangers watch one another die in horrible ways (axed in the head, crushed by a marble statue, and so on) as the novel counts down the survivors. None of Christie's beloved detectives are here to catch the criminal. Rather, a form of justice is meted out by someone with a warped sense of morality. No comic relief is provided, unlike in Christie's other works. Scholars and readers instead describe the book as existentially bleak; the only thing that seems to matter in the story is survival.

What accounts for this darker turn in Christie's fiction? It's thought that one anecdote from her autobiography provides a clue. Here she recounts an incident, occurring sometime between 1932 and 1933, where she discovered that acquaintances of hers and Max's, a married couple, were devoted Nazis. During a social gathering, the husband, a renowned physician and trained pianist, stated while playing the piano that Jewish citizens should be "exterminated" because they were "a danger." Christie wrote that the experience was deeply disturbing and stayed with her for years.

The More You Know

***And Then There Were None* has been adapted more than any other Christie novel. Among these adaptations is the 1945 acclaimed film version starring Walter Huston and Barry Fitzgerald. Full of Gothic atmosphere, it contains moments of comedy, unlike the book. However, reviewers noted that it still captures the suspense and despair of the original work.**

The Taxman Cometh

The 1930s were very productive years for Christie as a writer. Yet despite writing and publishing an average of one or more books per year, Agatha was worried about her financial situation. The trouble was taxes. In 1938, she received a letter from her UK agent, Edmund Cork, announcing that the IRS was asking questions about her finances. Agatha's American agent, Harold Ober, had engaged a prominent tax lawyer, Howard E. Reinheimer, to handle their inquiries.

Until 1938, Agatha had been classified in America as a "non-resident alien author." Under this category, tax on the sale of her copyrights was payable only in Britain. Then, the "Sabatini case" came along. Rafael Sabatini was a British citizen who made his income partly on American sales of his historical epics. In 1938, Sabatini's case ended with the ruling that he would pay US tax on the sale of his US copyrights. If a similar decision were reached in Christie's case, it would cost her as much as $78,500, Cork calculated (roughly $1,800,000 today).

Between buying houses and funding many of Max's expeditions to the Middle East, Agatha didn't have the money to pay this amount. If she were forced to give the IRS what Cork calculated, she'd be bankrupt. In August 1940, the IRS stopped export of her earnings until the tax matter was settled. By December, it appeared that anything Christie earned in the US would be withheld to offset an eventual settlement. This withholding went on for years as hearing after hearing was postponed. "The situation is pretty desperate with no money coming in," Cork wrote to Ober. By 1948, it looked as if Agatha would finally receive the American money the IRS owed her.

Then a new problem arose: The British revenue service didn't know how, or whether, to tax this sudden income. "What's the *good* of writing for money if I don't get *anything* out of it?" Agatha wrote Ober. In the wake of this issue, she decided to stop writing two books each year and to spend more time with family, as well as on her growing interest in archaeology and playwriting.

THE MORE YOU KNOW

Rafael Sabatini was an Italian-born British writer who specialized in romances and adventure novels. Like Christie, he was a bestselling, prolific novelist popular around the world. His most famous novel is *Captain Blood*, which was adapted in 1935 into a Hollywood film starring Errol Flynn and Olivia de Havilland.

"A Quite Unnecessary Fuss"

In 1937, as Agatha and Max continued to enjoy their married life, Rosalind turned eighteen. It was her debutante season. She had just returned from her travels to Switzerland, Paris, and Munich where, according to Agatha's plans for her, she learned French and gained a bit of cosmopolitan perspective. Unlike her mother, whose own debut was constrained by financial limitations, Rosalind had a lavish debutante season. Agatha had the means to provide one, though as a divorced woman, she was not allowed to present Rosalind at Buckingham Palace. That honor went to a friend, who got to witness Rosalind, dressed in ostrich feathers and a train, being greeted by King George VI.

When World War II broke out in 1939, shortly before the release of *And Then There Were None*, Rosalind was living at Greenway with Agatha and Max. One afternoon, she announced that in a few days' time she was going to marry a man named Hubert Prichard. Twelve years Rosalind's senior, he was an officer in the Royal Welch Fusiliers. In her autobiography, Agatha recounts the conversation between her and Rosalind about the wedding:

"I suppose you want to come to the wedding, Mother?"

"Of course I want to come to the wedding."

"I supposed you would. . . . But really it is a quite unnecessary fuss, I think. I mean, don't you think it would really be simpler for you and less tiring if you didn't?"

Rosalind and Hubert married in Denbigh, Wales, where he was stationed, on June 11, 1940. Agatha and Max were in attendance. Hubert then returned to the battlefield. In September 1943, Rosalind had a baby, Mathew, at a nursing home in Cheshire, close to Abney Hall, where Agatha's sister, Madge, lived. With Hubert gone, Agatha took Rosalind and Mathew back to London that fall. But the city proved too dangerous for a newborn (when the air raid alarms went off, Agatha and Rosalind would push baby Mathew in his "carry-cot" underneath a table with a thick glass top). Shortly afterward, Rosalind moved to Pwllywrach, Hubert's family estate in Wales, where Agatha would make frequent trips to visit them.

By 1944, life seemed settled for Rosalind, Agatha, and the baby. But across the ocean, in France, Hubert Prichard was landing in Normandy.

The More You Know

On June 6, 1944, the Allied forces launched a massive invasion to liberate Nazi-occupied France and other parts of Europe. Over 150,000 troops, along with five thousand ships and thousands of aircraft, landed on five different beaches in Normandy. The Battle of Normandy ultimately proved victorious for the Allies, but it cost the lives of nearly 75,000 of them.

From *A Daughter's a Daughter*, Chapter 1

Ann Prentice stood on the platform at Victoria, waving.

The boat train drew out in a series of purposeful jerks, Sarah's dark head disappeared, and Ann Prentice turned to walk slowly down the platform towards the exit.

She experienced the strangely mixed sensations that seeing a loved one off may occasionally engender.

Darling Sarah—how she would miss her. . . . Of course it was only for three weeks. . . . But the flat would seem so empty. . . . Just herself and Edith—two dull middle-aged women. . . .

Sarah was so alive, so vital, so positive about everything. . . . And yet still such a darling black-haired baby—

How awful! What a way to think! How frightfully annoyed Sarah would be! The one thing that Sarah—and all the other girls of her age—seemed to insist upon was an attitude of casual indifference on the part of their parents. "No *fuss*, Mother," they said urgently.

Christie At War

Many women of Christie's class, including her friends, had fled London to escape the bombings of the Second World War. Agatha, however, chose to remain in London, first in Sheffield Terrace in Notting Hill and then, after it was bombed in 1941, in the Isokon Building in Hampstead.

Max was stationed in the Middle East for most of the war, serving in the Air Ministry. In early 1942, he went to Cairo as a squadron leader. His knowledge of Arabic was useful, so the ministry also sent him to Tripolitania, Egypt, North Africa, and the Fezzan desert. From these places, Max wrote to Agatha about feeling useful: "I know I am doing a man's job, pulling my weight and not wasted."

Meanwhile, Christie worked two or three days a week at the pharmacy in University College Hospital dispensing drugs. And she wrote. The war years turned out to be her most prolific and productive writing period, in fact. During this time, she published ten novels, twenty stories, and one play. Among these was *Sad Cypress* (1940); *N or M?*, a 1941 Tommy and Tuppence spy novel; *Absent in the Spring* (1944), her favorite novel; and two Miss Marple novels, *The Body in the Library* (1942) and *The Moving Finger* (1942).

In her autobiography, Christie would describe the daily dangers she faced as a London resident during this time: "It had become . . . natural to expect that you yourself might be killed soon, that the people you loved best might be killed, that you would hear of deaths of friends. Broken windows, bombs, land mines, and in due course flying bombs and rockets—all these things would go on, not as something extraordinary, but as perfectly natural."

The war ended on September 2, 1945. Christie, her husband, daughter, and grandson all survived with no bodily harm. Agatha's sister, Madge, and Madge's husband, James, and son, Jack, all survived the war too, Madge having run Abney Hall—cleaning the hall's forty rooms, tending the kitchen and gardens—almost single-handedly when army officers billeted in the house. Life soon turned comfortable again for Agatha and her family. But scholars agree that after the war, her novels would be noticeably darker than those written before it. World War II, it seemed, had left its mark on the author.

LITERARY CONNECTIONS

The other Christie novels published during the war include *One, Two Buckle My Shoe* (1940), *Evil Under the Sun* (1941), *Five Little Pigs* (1942), *Death Comes As the End* (1944), and *Towards Zero* (1944).

Puper Dear

"Puper" was the nickname that Agatha and Max Mallowan had for each other, though no one seems to know how it originated. Much of their wartime correspondence began with "Puper Dear." These letters reveal a relationship marked by simple, ordinary pleasures like food and conversation. In one letter, Agatha writes, "What lovely times we will have when we are together again and how we shall eat!! There will be your socks with holes in them!! And things strewn everywhere and chairs covered with books and a lot of laughing—And we will talk and talk and talk."

Max's letters, though fewer than Agatha's, are tender and loving in tone. "What I treasure in you is your imagination," he writes in one letter. "That has been a continual stimulus to me, needful to the scholarly side, your love and affection without which life is a drab thing, your enthusiasm, freshness and vitality, your capacity for sharing my interests and enjoyments." Max deeply appreciated Agatha's involvement in his archaeological work. But he also admired her "imagination" and "enthusiasm": two qualities that biographers note her first husband, Archie, found irritating in his wife.

The letters also suggest that Agatha experienced insecurity about her marriage during these years. The couple spent long periods apart. Agatha even contacted her literary agent, Edmund Cork, at one point to see if *National Geographic* could commission some articles on Africa because Max was stationed there (the magazine refused). And while she was in London, where bombings were more and more common, she knew that Max was living in a house by the sea in Tripolitania, with the company of both male and female colleagues. As she wrote in one letter, "I had a horrid dream that I had come to visit you somewhere abroad. . . . They told me that you no longer cared or wanted me and had gone away and I woke up in a panic and had to say over and over—It's not true—it's not true—I've got his letter."

When Max did finally come home in the spring of 1945, he surprised Agatha by knocking on the door of their flat, as she would recount in her autobiography. "What on earth are you eating?" he asked when she opened the door. "Kippers," she answered. "You had better have one." And so, Max and Agatha went on with their life together.

THE MORE YOU KNOW

World War II led to a dramatic increase in the number of divorces throughout Britain. In 1938, roughly six thousand divorces were granted in the UK. In 1947, that number had jumped to sixty thousand: a tenfold increase. Historians cite prolonged separation, infidelity, the psychological impact of war, and the changing roles of women as central causes.

Tragedy

In many ways, 1944 had been a good year for Agatha. That January, her stage adaptation of *Death on the Nile*, *Hidden Horizon*, premiered at the Dundee Repertory Theatre in Scotland to good reviews. In June and July, *Towards Zero* was published in the US and UK. Then in August, as *Absent in the Spring* was released, a telegram came for Rosalind. It informed Rosalind that her husband was missing in France.

Agatha left London for Pwllywrach, where Rosalind and Mathew were now staying. Max was still in the Middle East. Agatha's letters to Max at this time describe how Rosalind continued in her responsibilities following the news: "It is terrible for Ros. She is wonderful—never turns a hair—carries on exactly as usual—with food, dogs, Mathew—we act as though nothing has happened." But as weeks continued to pass with no word on Hubert, Pwllywrach, once a grand manor house, was falling into decay. The constant repairs it needed began to overwhelm Rosalind, according to biographers.

Agatha's third novel that year to be published, *Death Comes As the End*, came out in October 1944. That same month, Rosalind learned that her husband had been killed in action. He had died on August 16 at Les Loges-Saulces in Calvados, France, leading a rescue operation to pick up some men who'd been ambushed. Before Hubert was able to get to them, his tank blew up. "A gallant but thoughtless act," wrote his colonel. Now twenty-five years old, Rosalind Prichard was a widow, and her two-year-old son, Mathew, was fatherless. "Rosalind lets it make no difference to her—took Mathew out to tea with some people as arranged—eats her meals well and calmly makes arrangements about obituary notices, etc. That stoical temperament is wonderful," Agatha wrote in another letter to Max.

At the end of October, Agatha returned to London. Meanwhile, Rosalind and her son continued to live in Pwllywrach. Presumably, Rosalind saw or at least corresponded with her father, Archie Christie, during this time. As she would recount in 1990 for an interview with *The Times*, "I saw him often, and we always liked and understood one another." Archie had now been married to Nancy Neele for nearly twenty years, and while Rosalind apparently made it a point to avoid her stepmother as much as possible, she and her father remained close.

LITERARY CONNECTIONS

Dilapidated country estates such as Pwllywrach abound in Agatha's fiction. Examples include Rutherford Hall in *4:50 from Paddington* and Styles in *Curtain*. These lines from *Paddington* illustrate the economic pressure of maintaining large estates: "The kitchen garden was sketchily cultivated with a few vegetables. The hot-houses were in ruins. The paths everywhere were overgrown with weeds."

Postwar Agatha

After the war, Max and Agatha got on with their lives. Agatha quit the dispensary, and Max landed a position at the University of London in 1947, resuming his archaeological digs in 1949. Agatha loved being a grandmother to Mathew, and her relationship with her daughter started to improve now that Rosalind depended on Agatha for advice about domestic matters and help with childcare.

Agatha was fifty-five and, as she would recall, tired of living in a London flat and always working. She wished to be back in Devon. On Christmas Day, 1945, she got her wish: Greenway, which had been taken over by the Admiralty during the war, was derequisitioned. After four years without gardeners or handymen, Greenway needed mending, and Agatha immediately got to work. During the time that fifty-one American soldiers had been living in Greenway, the library had been converted to a messroom, and there a soldier had painted a massive fresco depicting all the places—Key West, Morocco, etc.—that their flotilla (fleet of ships) had visited. At the edge of the fresco was a "pin-up girl in the nude," as Agatha later described it. The Navy offered to paint over the fresco, but Agatha "hurriedly replied that it would be an historic memorial, and that I was delighted to have it." She did, however, convert the room back into a library.

Greenway soon became a holiday house. Rosalind, Mathew, and Rosalind's second husband, Anthony Arthur Hicks, visited every summer. Rosalind had met Hicks in Somerset while traveling, and they married soon afterward in October 1949. By all accounts, this second marriage was a happy one, Anthony fitting into the family easily with his charm, curiosity, and devotion to Agatha and Max.

LITERARY CONNECTIONS

Friends and relatives would also come to Greenway for weeks at a time, playing cricket on the lawn and eating Christie's lobster thermidor. The novelist Edmund Crispin, a favorite guest of the couple's, described Greenway as "very informal. There was a massive dining room and you never knew what you were going to get. You might be eating off Georgian silver or something from Woolworth's. You might be pouring wine from an eighteenth-century port decanter or drinking from some cheap glasses Agatha had found when shopping. There were children and dogs and always amusing talk."

From Crooked House, Chapter 4

"It's very important, Charles, that I should make you understand this. You see, we're a very queer family. . . . There's a lot of ruthlessness in us—and—different kinds of ruthlessness. That's what's so disturbing. The different kinds."

She must have seen incomprehension in my face. She went on, speaking energetically.

"I'll try and make what I mean clear. Grandfather, for instance. Once, when he was telling us about his boyhood in Smyrna, he mentioned, quite casually, that he had stabbed two men. It was some kind of a brawl—there had been some unforgiveable insult—I don't know—but it was just a thing that happened quite naturally. He'd really practically forgotten about it. But it was, somehow, such a queer thing to hear about, quite casually, in England."

Becoming a Brand

Christie continued to write, though at a slower pace. From now on, she would average one detective book a year, each scheduled for release during the holiday season: "A Christie for Christmas," Collins called it. In 1946, Christie published *The Hollow*, the first novel in four years to feature Poirot (though later she claimed his presence "ruined" the book). In 1948, she published *Taken at the Flood*, which explores the economic challenges facing a small village after the war. That same year, *The Rose and the Yew Tree*, Agatha's fourth Mary Westmacott novel, appeared in print.

And in 1950, Collins released *A Murder Is Announced*, Agatha's fifth Marple book. Often considered the best of all the Marple novels, it is set in the classic (though fictional) English village of Chipping Cleghorn, where the residents read an ad announcing that a murder will take place that night at a party. They all attend out of idle curiosity—but indeed, much to their horror, an actual murder occurs. Collins ran a big publicity campaign for the book, as it was the author's fiftieth book if counting short story collections—and she herself was turning sixty that year.

As scholars have noted, Agatha Christie was no longer an author at this time, but a *brand*. Two years before, she had broken all publishing records when 100,000 copies of ten of her titles—or a million novels—were all released by Penguin on the same day. A Christie for Christmas had sealed this branding, reinforcing how readers had come to expect a certain kind of mystery from the author. Christie rarely gave interviews, but her image as a conventional, ordinary woman who happened to write murder novels was now firmly solidified as she approached old age.

That August, just before Agatha's birthday and the attendant celebrations, her beloved sister, Madge, died of heart disease at a hospital in Manchester. She was seventy-one years old. Christie learned of the news while vacationing at Greenway. Frederick, Clara, Monty, and now Madge were all gone. She was the only one of that family left.

LITERARY CONNECTIONS

Other Christie works written and published between 1945 and 1950 include *Sparkling Cyanide* (1945), her last novel to feature Colonel Race (an ex-military man who helps detectives with their cases), and *Crooked House* (1949), which depicts a case of murder by poison (an eserine-based eye medicine, administered by an insulin injection!).

Agatha Christie, Archaeologist

Life with Max during the 1930s had introduced Agatha to many new places. But would these adventures carry on now that the war was over? Would Max be able to continue his excavations in the Middle East? The answer to these questions came in 1947, when Max was appointed to the first chair in Western Asiatic Archaeology at the Institute of Archaeology in the University of London. The position, along with Agatha's supplemental funding, enabled Max to begin a new expedition to Nimrud, an ancient Assyrian city located in Iraq. From 1949 to 1959, Max dug at Nimrud each year. According to archaeologist John Curtis, Max's team made some extraordinary, well-publicized discoveries, including two ivory female heads, one nicknamed the "Mona Lisa," the other "Ugly Sister."

The first month of the Mallowans' annual trips to Nimrud was always spent in Baghdad, where the couple stayed at the house of the British School of Archaeology. It was an old house, full of windows. Each morning, Agatha would sit on one of the balconies and have a breakfast of toast, marmalade, and pomegranate juice, hand squeezed for her by the cook.

Following their month in Baghdad, she and Max would proceed to the excavation site. Agatha would later describe how she loved Nimrud—its unusual flowers and birds, its tranquility, its desert sublimity—and enjoyed helping Max manage the staff and local workers. On the expeditions, she made sure there was always fresh food to eat, insisting that the cooks use local produce whenever possible, and created recipes for eclairs with cream from water buffalo and chocolate soufflés cooked in a tin box, often doing the cooking herself.

Max's expeditions were small, and Agatha served as an important member of his team. She took almost all the photographs of their archaeological finds, for example, and developed the images herself. With her favorite tools, orange sticks and Innoxa face cream, she removed the dust and dirt from ivory fragments and took the hundreds of ivory bits Max and his team uncovered and reassembled them into their original forms. During these expeditions, Agatha also wrote steadily, producing works such as *They Came to Baghdad* (1951), a spy novel set in the city she and Max visited before each trip to Nimrud.

LITERARY CONNECTIONS

In November 1946, Christie published a book, *Come, Tell Me How You Live,* under her married name, Mallowan. A humorous memoir about her adventures with Max on archaeological digs during the 1930s, it was initially rejected in 1944 by Collins, who were suspicious of anything that took time away from the detective fiction that was so lucrative. The book, however, sold well.

Agatha Christie and the Charge of Racism

In 1947, Christie's literary agent Edmund Cork received a letter from the Anti-Defamation League (ADL), an American organization founded in 1913 to combat anti-Semitism and other forms of prejudice. The letter expressed outrage at Christie's use of slurs regarding Jews and racial minorities, demanding that all such language be expunged from new editions of her novels. Indeed, derogatory words and phrases had been included in Christie's fiction since 1920, when she published *The Mysterious Affair at Styles*. Such language was usually voiced by villainous or dislikable characters. Still, the phrasing was criticized, and Christie responded to the letter by giving permission to Dodd, Mead & Co., her US publishers, to remove all derogatory language and situations from her books.

The letter from the ADL wasn't the first instance of racist accusations against Christie. The original title of *And Then There Were None* included a slur of Black citizens. Christie had borrowed the title from an 1869 British children's doggerel (comic poem verse) and also named the island setting of the novel after this term. While Collins, her British publisher, continued to release the novel under its original title until 1985, Dodd, Mead & Co., Christie's American publishers, released the novel in 1940 as *And Then There Were None,* the last, chilling line of the original doggerel.

When a stage adaptation of the novel premiered at the Broadhurst Theater on Broadway in June 1944, it ran under the title *Ten Little Indians.* Why producers switched to this title is unclear, but the play was a huge success (it ran for almost a full year), and future American producers retained the title for their own adaptations. Pocket Books, issuing a paperback version of the novel in 1964, also used this title.

Biographers and scholars argue that Christie was a product of her age and upbringing—and that the entertainment and publishing industries have been as much to blame in these incidents as the author. They also point out that during World War II, while she was living in the Isokon Building, Christie had befriended many Jewish refugees. She was coming to understand the horrors that racial prejudice can produce, and while her later works still contained potentially offensive language and situations on occasion, they would reflect a general shift in the author's representation of non-white characters.

THE MORE YOU KNOW

Originally an American counting rhyme, "Ten Little Indians" was adapted in 1868 by American songwriter Septimus Winner as the song "Ten Little Injuns" for a minstrel show. Most scholars believe it preceded the 1869 British doggerel that included a racial slur, though the doggerel's origin remains unclear.

Agatha Christie Ltd.

In 1948, a settlement was reached regarding the back taxes Christie owed to the IRS. She would have to give a total of $160,000 (the equivalent of roughly $2 million today) for the years 1930–1941, plus legal and accountancy fees.

More bad news followed quickly. The English government was staking a claim to the remainder of Christie's American income, frozen for a decade and now returned to her. Surtax was notably high in the late 1940s and 1950s, the result of Britain's efforts to rebuild its welfare state. On top of what she owed the IRS, she now had to pay over 70,000 pounds (somewhere between 2 and 2.5 million pounds today) to the British revenue service. Cork had saved up money for Christie during these years but feared the worst for his client. "There seems to be little likelihood of Mrs. Mallowan avoiding bankruptcy," he wrote to Harold Ober, Christie's American agent.

It turned out that Christie *did* avoid bankruptcy, but there were questions about what would happen regarding her taxes in the future. She was set to make more money in the years ahead; how much would she owe on that income, and how would she pay it? "I think something ought to be done and quickly," Cork wrote to Ober. Their solution was the Christie Settlement Trust, founded in 1955. The arrangement went as follows: Christie gave the trustees 100 pounds, which they used to purchase one hundred shares in a company: Agatha Christie Ltd. From this point forward, the company would employ Christie to write her novels and pay her a salary. Two years later, in January 1957, another trust was formed, the Christie Copyrights Trust, to oversee the copyrights of works Christie had completed before the creation of the company.

This new arrangement meant that Christie had to give away a lot of money in ways of her choosing, rather than handing it over to the IRS or the British revenue service. Relatives and friends who needed help received money from time to time, as did a host of different charities, including the Harrison Homes, which provided housing for old people who needed a safe and affordable place to live.

Bankruptcy had been avoided—but Christie would continue to have financial worries for the rest of her life. (More on this later.)

THE MORE YOU KNOW

Richard Burton, The Rolling Stones, Rod Stewart, and David Bowie, among other celebrities, left the UK for periods of time because of high taxation: something Christie refused to do. The Rolling Stones, in fact, called themselves "Tax Exiles." Like Agatha, The Beatles formed a company, named Northern Songs (to which they sold their music rights), as a strategy for avoiding bankruptcy.

The Fans

By 1950, Christie had reached the height of her popularity. Her novels were selling fifty thousand or more copies within the first few weeks. Numbering among Christie's millions of fans were Queen Elizabeth II, Woodrow Wilson, and Albert Einstein. Many of her fans wrote letters to Christie. She kept this correspondence, answering much of it personally. In 2015, as part of the commemorations of the 125th anniversary of Christie's birth, a collection of this fan mail was published.

Sometimes, fan correspondence contained strange, even comic, requests. Some people wrote asking for money ("Please do be an angel and help me"). One man wrote to declare, "I admire you and respect you and love you, Miss Christie, more than anything in the world." And in the 1960s, decades before such a project became commonplace, a computer expert asked for help with his digital compilation on "Mrs. Marple's life."

In 1972, when Christie was in her eighties, she received a letter from Shirley Dawson, a teenage girl in Florida who wrote her own mysteries. Christie replied, "Try out different ways—different kinds of stories." When Dawson wrote again, expressing concern that readers might copycat her criminal methods, Christie answered a second time, "I think your instinct is quite right in not caring to use ideas for crimes which might suggest methods to those who have criminal tendencies."

Many fans wrote about their love of Christie novels. One boy from Bristol, writing in 1958, explained that he had started a "Crime Club" at his school. "Since then, I have bought 28 books by you and this is how I have managed it. I charged the boys 3d per book to read at school, and 6d if they wished to take them home. . . . Now my scheme is bringing in so much money that I can afford to buy one of your books a week." (The terms "3d" and "6d" refer to 3 and 6 pence, respectively.) And a Polish woman recounted how one of Christie's novels helped her survive a labor camp during World War II. She had exchanged a piece of candle for a Polish translation of *The Man in the Brown Suit*. "I read and re-read it so often that I almost knew it by heart. . . . Never can one of your books have meant more to anyone than that tattered Polish translation did to me."

The More You Know

Despite her widespread fanbase, no formal society or club devoted to Agatha Christie existed until 1993. That year, Agatha Christie Ltd. founded the Agatha Christie Society. Its first president was Agatha's daughter, Rosalind Hicks, with David Suchet and Joan Hickson, the British actors who played Poirot and Miss Marple, respectively, on television, serving as vice presidents. The society closed in 2003.

The Critics

Not everyone has been a fan of Agatha Christie. Among her most famous detractors was Raymond Chandler, the American writer known for novels such as *The Big Sleep* and *The Long Goodbye*. In December 1944, Chandler published an essay, "The Simple Art of Murder," in *The Atlantic*, where he excoriated Golden Age detective writers, Christie in particular. In his view, their fiction had nothing to do with real crime or criminals. Nor was their skill at "puzzle mysteries" any good: "They [Golden Age novels] are too contrived, and too little aware of what goes on in the world." Of *And Then There Were None*, Agatha's bestselling and most acclaimed novel, Chandler declared, "It is as complete and shameless a bamboozling of the reader as ever was perpetrated."

Chandler's essay followed another widely read article, "Why Do People Read Detective Stories?" published in *The New Yorker* on October 6, 1944. The author, Edmund Wilson, recounts his decision to read "new novels particularly esteemed by connoisseurs" of detective fiction to learn the reason for the genre's popularity. His verdict: "You cannot read such a book. You run through it to see the problem worked out; and you cannot become interested in the characters because they can never be allowed an existence of their own." According to Wilson, the popularity of these novels is not due to artistic merit but to a postwar need for reassurance that good will triumph over evil.

Other Christie detractors include Robert Graves, the author of *I, Claudius* and a friend of Christie's, who said, "Nobody could promise Agatha immortality as a novelist. Her English is school-girlish, her situations for the most part artificial, her detail faulty." Years later, British crime writer Michael Dibdin remarked, "Her aim was to fool the readers, and she sacrificed everything to achieve it. The plots in Christie's novels were all basically the same. . . . The characters were all generalized types. . . . Her books were artificially pure, and she ignored the problems faced by society." Novelist Frances Wyndham called Christie's novels "animated algebra," and crime writer Julian Symons termed them "riddles rather than books."

According to Rosalind and Max Mallowan, these criticisms didn't seem to bother Christie in the least. She claimed all her life that she wrote to entertain and that she thought of herself as "a tradesman—a tradesman in a good honest trade."

LITERARY CONNECTIONS

Raymond Chandler was one of the "hard-boiled" school of writers popular in the 1920s–1940s. Arguing that Golden Age novels were too genteel and cerebral, these writers promoted their work as tough, unsentimental, and realistic. Other hard-boiled writers include Dashiell Hammett, James M. Cain, Mignon Good Eberhart and Harriette Ashbrook.

From Dead Man's Folly, Chapter 17

"It's splendid that you've wrung me up," she said. "I was just going out to give a talk on 'How I Write My Books.' Now I can get my secretary to ring up and say I am unavoidably detained."

"But, Madame, you must not let me prevent—"

"It's not a case of preventing," said Mrs. Oliver joyfully. "I'd have made the most awful fool of myself. I mean, what can you say about how you write books? What I mean is, first you've got to think of something, and when you've thought of it you've got to force yourself to sit down and write it. That's all. It would have taken me just three minutes to explain that, and then the TALK would have ended and everyone would have been very fed up. I can't imagine why everybody is always so keen for authors to talk about writing. I should have thought it was an author's business to *write*, not *talk*."

Drama Queen, Act 2

For Christie, getting one of her plays produced had been a frustrating experience. Throughout the 1930s, she had to contend with producers who were only interested in putting on Christie plays that featured Poirot. What's more, her theatrical adaptation of her story "Philomel Cottage" never came to light, though Frank Vosper, who wrote and staged his own version of the story in 1936, lifted material heavily from it without crediting it (he credited the story, not the play). Two other plays written in the 1930s, *Akhnaton,* a historical drama, and *A Daughter's a Daughter,* didn't get produced until decades later (*Akhnaton* in 1973 and *A Daughter's A Daughter* in 1956).

In 1943, her adaptation of *And Then There Were None* was a commercial hit in the West End. A year later, in 1944, the Shuberts opened their wildly successful production, *Ten Little Indians,* on Broadway. Complex negotiations and poor performances, however, hobbled other Christie plays. *Appointment with Death,* which premiered in the West End on March 31, 1945, closed after forty-two performances (by comparison, *And Then There Were None* ran for 260 performances in the West End and 426 on Broadway). Christie's adaptation of *Towards Zero,* highly sought after due to the novel's powerhouse sales and specially commissioned by the

Shuberts for a Broadway run, never got produced because of trouble with the third act.

In March 1946, *Murder on the Nile,* Christie's adaptation of *Death on the Nile,* tanked in the West End. *Hidden Horizon,* also an adaptation of *Death on the Nile,* premiered on Broadway later that year and closed after just twelve performances.

According to Julius Green, Christie's critical reputation as a playwright was now "in tatters on both sides of the Atlantic." Then, in 1949, Christie met Peter Saunders, the man who would soon become the architect of her theatrical career. In 1951, he arranged for her adaptation of *The Hollow,* a 1946 novel featuring Poirot, to be produced in the West End.

Audiences loved *The Hollow,* even though Poirot had been cut from the play's storyline. Agatha's belief that her books would do better on stage without Poirot, after years of being told otherwise, finally proved right. And at age sixty-one, Agatha found an encore career.

LITERARY CONNECTIONS

The detective replacing Poirot in the play is Inspector Colquhoun, aided by Detective Sergeant Penny. Neither detective appears in any other work of Christie's. Elaborating on these characters, Christie explained to her audience that "I have tried to make my detective as natural as possible, both in himself and in his methods. After all the 'private investigator' isn't much known in real life, apart from divorce matters."

The Queen's Birthday Present

In 1947, while Christie was attempting to advance her work as a playwright, the UK's Queen Mary was turning eighty years old. When the BBC asked her how it could celebrate her birthday, the queen replied that she'd like a radio play written by her favorite author, Agatha Christie. Christie agreed, turning to real life for ideas. Her inspiration was the Dennis O'Neill case, which made headlines for most of 1945. Twelve-year-old O'Neill and his younger brothers, Terence, age nine, and Frederick, age seven, had been placed under foster protection and were sent to live with Reginald and Esther Gough in Shropshire, England.

In January 1945, Esther Gough telephoned a doctor to say that Dennis was "having a fit." The doctor arrived an hour later to find Dennis dead. An inquest followed, in which it was determined that the boy had suffered cardiac arrest from heavy blows to his chest and back. Reginald and Esther Gough were subsequently charged with manslaughter.

Christie's spin on this case was to focus on one of the younger, surviving brothers. In her play, he is now a grown man, seeking vengeance on the couple who killed his brother. The husband has since died, but the wife has abused and killed other children in the interim. Before the play begins, the surviving brother has already murdered the wife in London—but he takes refuge from the police in a boardinghouse where eight other guests reside. A blinding snowstorm traps them all inside the house, and murder ensues. This was the story that became *Three Blind Mice*, broadcast by the BBC as a twenty-minute play on May 30, 1947, as part of an evening of programming honoring the queen's eightieth birthday. The play's title was one of many works by Christie—*Five Little Pigs*; *One, Two, Buckle My Shoe*; *Hickory Dickory Dock*—that came from a nursery rhyme.

After the triumph of *The Hollow*, Christie would decide to adapt *Three Blind Mice* into a full-length play in 1952. However, another play with the same title had run in the West End earlier, so Peter Saunders came up with a new title for the adaptation: *The Mousetrap*. This title was taken from a description by Shakespeare's Hamlet about a play he has designed to trap Claudius's conscience. *The Mousetrap* would become the world's longest-running theatrical production.

The More You Know

Until the O'Neill case, newspaper coverage of child abuse cases was scarce. Furthermore, police and physicians tended to dismiss the cases they saw, believing parents who claimed their child's injuries were the result of accidents. After the O'Neill case, however, physicians and radiologists began using X-rays to locate discrepancies between parental statements and the injuries themselves.

Humor and Thriller Appeal

The Mousetrap opened on November 25, 1952, at the Ambassadors Theatre. Audience members were given a program picturing a mousetrap against a splash of red. By all accounts, excitement was high that night not only because *The Mousetrap* was an Agatha Christie production but also because it starred two of the West End's stars: Richard Attenborough (voted Britain's sixth most popular actor in 1949) and his wife, Sheila Sim. Adding to the excitement, the manager appeared onstage just before the curtain went up, urging the audience not to reveal the plot twist at the end.

Reviews of *The Mousetrap* were glowing. *Punch* magazine called it "one of Mrs. Christie's neatest puzzles and it takes to the stage very naturally." When the play opened in America, *Variety* reported, "Final thriller of the year is this ingenious whodunit by Agatha Christie, whose *The Hollow* last year swung the trend back to worthwhile crime plays." On premiere night in London, Christie predicted an eight-month run for the play. However, it has run continuously for over seven decades. Reflecting on its success in her autobiography, Christie would write: "I think, considering it and trying to be neither conceited nor over-modest that, of its kind—which is to say a light play with both humor and thriller appeal—it is well constructed. The thing unfolds so that you want to know what happens next, and you can't quite see where the next few minutes will lead you."

According to theater historian Julius Green, the play's longevity has attracted both praise and critique, with some critics arguing that *The Mousetrap*'s astoundingly long run is less a mark of its artistic merit than the West End's reluctance to try out new, unknown plays and directors. Regardless, with over thirty thousand performances to date, *The Mousetrap* has generated an estimated $1 billion in the West End alone. Christie bestowed the rights to the play on Mathew, her grandson, just before his ninth birthday. "Mathew," she'd later say, "was always the most lucky member of the family."

The More You Know

No film adaptation has ever been made of *The Mousetrap*. Under the contract terms of the play, a film version can't be produced until the West End production has been closed for at least six months (the play shut down from March 2020 to May 2021 during the COVID-19 pandemic, but it didn't close). In the UK, copies of Christie's short story "Three Blind Mice" aren't available to the public due to another contract condition, stating that the story cannot be published while the play is running in the West End.

From The Mousetrap, Act 1

VOICE ON THE RADIO. "And according to Scotland Yard, the crime took place at twenty-four Culver Street, Paddington. The murdered woman was a Mrs. Maureen Lyon. In connection with the murder, the police—" (MOLLIE rises and crosses to the armchair centre.)

"—are anxious to interview a man seen in the vicinity, wearing a dark overcoat—"

(MOLLIE picks up Giles's overcoat.)

"—light scarf—" (MOLLIE picks up Giles's scarf.)

"—and a soft felt hat."

(MOLLIE picks up his hat and exits through the arch up right.)

"Motorists are warned against ice-bound roads."

(The door bell rings.)

"The heavy snow is expected to continue, and throughout the country . . ."

Agatha versus the Angries

As Agatha Christie's playwriting career thrived, sales of her novels continued to skyrocket in the 1950s. But her literary reputation began its steady decline. This was in part because the 1950s marked the decade of new writers such as John Osborne, Philip Larkin, and Patricia Highsmith, who were experimental in their use of form and tended to be scathing in their portraits of pre- and postwar Britain, especially its institutions. Their tone veers toward cynicism, sometimes anger and disgust. Many of these writers, a group dubbed the "Angry Young Men," or less commonly the "Angries," were young males claiming to be part of the working class. Others, like Larkin and Highsmith, were gay. Both in their writing and in person, they were a contrast to Agatha Christie.

Christie was now beginning to be seen by critics as not only old-fashioned but also politically offensive. Accusations of anti-Semitism and racial prejudice returned, citing newer examples of offensive phrasing and characterizations in her writing. Eventually, the Council Against Intolerance in America stepped in, requesting that Dodd, Mead & Co. expunge all traces of anti-Semitism from new US editions of Christie's works.

But Christie's fiction did in fact change following the war. As scholars would note, her novels now conveyed a climate of paranoia and suspicion: Neighbors, once friendly, watch one another closely; people turn inward as they guard their secrets; servants, once dependable, are resentful; children kill. In *After the Funeral*, published in 1953, Miss Gilchrist resents her job as a paid companion to the wealthy Cora Lansquenet. Gilchrist had once been the owner of a tea shop, but due to wartime rationing, she became unable to get the eggs needed to bake cakes. Having lost her shop, she turns to murder—with a hatchet!

Despite this change in her writing, the idea of Agatha Christie as a "cozy" writer persisted. The public was too invested in the Christie brand. And just as later TV adaptations would do, her plays in the West End and Broadway, described by Agatha herself as "light" entertainment, reinforced this brand.

LITERARY CONNECTIONS

In *A Murder Is Announced*, published in 1950, Agatha portrays Mitzi, a refugee from Nazi Germany, as a comic figure. Terrified of the police when they try to question her about a murder, she says, in a way intended to make her sound comically paranoid, "You will send me away to a concentration camp."

The Quadruple Twist

While *The Mousetrap* may be Agatha's bestselling play, *Witness for the Prosecution* is considered by many to be her masterpiece. A three-act courtroom drama with four plot twists, it originated as a story first published by Christie as "Traitor Hands" in January 1925. The story's protagonist is Leonard Vole, the secret companion of a wealthy woman who is found dead one morning.

During the summer of 1951, twenty-six years after the story was published, Peter Saunders obtained the rights and convinced Christie to adapt it for the stage. For the play, she restructured the drama to take place in a courtroom. She also invented the character of Sir Wilfred Robarts, who represents Vole's defense; made Vole more charming than in the original story; and turned Romaine into an East German. Consulting legal experts, she researched how trials were conducted in the Central Criminal Court of England and Wales (also called the "Old Bailey"). Most notably, Christie changed the ending, adding a fourth and final twist to the play (what critics would call the "quadruple twist").

Witness opened at the Winter Garden Theatre on October 28, 1953. The first night was a triumph. Years later, Saunders wrote about the success: "If I had to choose my supreme moment in my theatre life this was it. . . . After innumerable curtain calls . . . the cast turned to the upper box where Agatha was sitting, and the entire company bowed. There was pandemonium in the theatre. Not only clapping and shouting, but people standing and waving. I have never in my life been at any theatre and heard such a reception. . . . As she left, she [Christie] whispered to me the understatement of all time, 'It's rather fun, isn't it?'" However restrained her comments, this night would be deeply memorable for Agatha: "So I was happy, radiantly happy. . . . My self-consciousness and nervousness, just for once, were not with me. Yes, it was a memorable evening. I am proud of it still. And every now and then I dig into the memory chest, bring it out, take a look at it, and say 'That was the night, that was!'"

LITERARY CONNECTIONS

The four twists of *Witness for the Prosecution* are (spoiler alert!): 1. Romaine gives damning testimony against Leonard Vole. 2. A surprise witness produces letters confirming that the adulterous Romaine tried to frame Vole for Emily French's murder. 3. After the trial, Romaine admits fabricating the letters, disguising herself as the surprise witness and lying under oath, knowing the jury might acquit a man with a scheming wife. 4. After he's acquitted, Vole tells Romaine he is leaving her; in response, she pulls out a gun and kills him.

From Witness for the Prosecution, Act 3

SIR WILFRID. (*Thunderstruck.*) "My God!"

ROMAINE. "Yes, the woman with the letters. I wrote those letters. I brought them to you. It wasn't *you* who won freedom for Leonard. It was I. And because of it I shall go to prison. But at the end of it Leonard and I will be together again. Happy—loving each other."

SIR WILFRID. (*Moved.*) "My dear . . . but couldn't you trust me? We believe, you know, that our British system of justice upholds the truth. We'd have gotten him off."

ROMAINE. "I couldn't risk it. (*Slowly.*) You see, you *thought* he was innocent . . ."

(Sir Wilfred *responds with quick appreciation.*)

SIR WILFRID. "And you *know* he was innocent. I understand."

ROMAINE. "But you do not understand at all. *I* knew he was *guilty.*"

"Parry and Punch"

Sometime in 1955, while *Witness for the Prosecution* was still playing on Broadway, Harold Ober, Agatha's American agent, announced that he was asking $450,000 for the film rights to the play. Gilbert Miller, a co-producer of the play, bought the rights for $325,000, then film producer Edward Small bought them from Miller for $430,000; Small then teamed with an independent producer named Arthur Hornblow to produce the film.

It was Hornblow who gave Billy Wilder, the legendary director, his first chance to direct a Hollywood film (for Paramount) in 1942. And when Marlene Dietrich said she'd only star in the film if Wilder directed it, Hornblow hired him to direct *Witness*. Wilder, who'd made his name with noir classics like *Double Indemnity* and *Sunset Boulevard*, was a huge fan of Christie's novels.

Once Wilder wrote the script, Hornblow gave it a large budget, employing 145 extras and thirty-eight stuntmen, for example, for just one scene. And in addition to casting Dietrich as Christine Vole, Hornblow selected then-heartthrob Tyrone Power to play Leonard Vole. Charles Laughton, the actor who nearly thirty years earlier had starred as Hercule Poirot in *Alibi*, would play the part of Robarts.

The story's twist ending was a vital part of the production and publicity for *Witness.* Wilder wouldn't let any of the cast members read the script's last ten pages; and at the end of the movie, as the credits rolled, a voiceover asked viewers not to share the twist with anyone who hadn't yet seen the movie. Posters for the film declared, "You'll talk about it!—but please don't tell the ending!"

Witness reigned No. 1 at the US box office for two consecutive weeks in February and March 1958 and secured six Academy Award nominations that year, including Best Picture. *The New York Times* wrote a glowing review and, by all accounts, Christie loved Wilder's adaptation of *Witness.*

In a few years, however, she would see a new stream of film adaptations that, in her view, ridiculed Miss Marple and the kind of crime fiction her creator wrote.

THE MORE YOU KNOW

***Witness for the Prosecution* was the last film completed by Tyrone Power, who died of a heart attack at age forty-four while shooting the movie *Solomon and Sheba* in 1958. Cast principally in adventure films (or "swashbucklers") because of his matinee-idol looks, Powers tried for years to break into more serious roles. *Witness* gave him such a role, casting him against type as an oily, despicable antagonist.**

The Case of MGM versus Christie

During the late 1950s and early 1960s, Agatha continued to write plays, including *Verdict*, *The Patient*, and *Go Back for Murder*. At The Savoy, with over a thousand people in attendance, *The Mousetrap* celebrated its record, in Julius Green's words, "as the longest-running production of any kind in the history of British theatre." Agatha and Max had stopped journeying to Iraq, while Rosalind was reportedly happy with her second husband, Anthony. Agatha's grandson, Mathew, would be soon heading off to university. In 1961, UNESCO declared Agatha Christie the bestselling author of all time. Except for a minor stroke Max suffered in 1962, all was well during these years.

And then MGM acquired the rights to adapt Christie's work. For nearly twenty-five years, the studio had been asking Edmund Cork about the rights. Under Agatha's instructions, Cork repeatedly turned them down. Recently, however, Cork hoped the income Christie would receive from this sale would end her tax worries once and for all. Christie finally agreed, and negotiations were finalized in 1960. Agatha said to Cork, "I hope there won't be broken hearts. What one loses in cash one may gain in absence of worry." Cork himself said of the negotiations, "The MGM deal has almost destroyed me, its fluctuations have been too numerous and violent to be believed."

The agreement gave the studio rights to forty of Agatha's stories on a profit-sharing agreement. MGM's initial plan was to do a TV series based on Miss Marple. But later in the year, the studio decided to debut the character on the big screen; if the film did well, MGM would then produce several TV series from Christie's work.

The first MGM film, *Murder She Said* (1961), was a loose adaptation of *4:50 from Paddington*. A "crime comedy," it gave Miss Marple a more humorous and active role than she had in the book. Of the change, one screenwriter explained, "The Miss Marple of the books struck me as snobbish, unkind and cold. . . . The intention with the screen Miss Marple was to create a person of warmth and gusto."

Viewers loved the movie. *The Illustrated London News* called it "a joy. Snorting, severe, permanently indignant yet permanently dignified, she [MGM's Miss Marple] is anyone's idea of an English great-aunt." Lawrence P. Bachmann, MGM's head of its British division, remarked in an interview that the film was "an exceptionally satisfactory money spinner." Christie, however, hated the adaptation. (More on this later.)

LITERARY CONNECTIONS

The MGM films were such a hit that publishers across the world used the image of Margaret Rutherford, who played Miss Marple, as a tie-in for Christie novels during the 1960s. Some even published *4:50 from Paddington* as *Murder She Said*.

Acting with Her Chin

At first, MGM producers imagined a younger actress for the role of Miss Marple. But by the end of 1960, just before production on *Murder She Said* started, they agreed on an older actress for the part: Margaret Rutherford.

A British character actress of stage, film, and television, Rutherford took up acting in her thirties. At thirty-three, she was cast in her first major play, acting as comic relief. She then made her name as Madame Arcati in the stage and screen versions of Noël Coward's *Blithe Spirit* during the early 1940s. Theater and film critics alike praised her humor and physicality. Legendary critic Kenneth Tynan once remarked, "The unique thing about Margaret Rutherford is that she can act with her chin alone."

Rutherford's success with *Blithe Spirit* led to many comedies in the late 1940s and 1950s in which she played characters described as lovably eccentric. Her theatrical voice ("half commanding schoolmistress, half bewildered storyteller," as one critic noted) also meant she was in high demand as a reader of children's stories on television. (She also read poetry all over England, including in "her majesty's jails.") In 1963, she won an Academy Award for Best Supporting

Actress for her role in *The V.I.P.s,* starring Maggie Smith, Richard Burton, and Elizabeth Taylor.

Rutherford was reportedly delighted to accept the part of Miss Marple. Although Christie would say she found Rutherford's performance very different from the character she had created, she admitted the actress was a talented comedian and wrote a short note to tell her so. "I can assure you that this is one of the proudest moments of my life," Rutherford replied in a long letter back to the author. Biographers consider it a troubling letter to read, for while the actress wrote that she hoped to continue in the role, Christie was attempting to get the films stopped. Still, Christie dedicated her 1962 novel, *The Mirror Crack'd from Side to Side,* to Rutherford "in admiration."

LITERARY CONNECTIONS

The Mirror Crack'd from Side to Side **is about a film star who leaves Hollywood and returns to England. She takes over Gossington Hall, the former residence of Miss Marple's friend Dolly Bantry. Scholars argue that Christie dedicated the novel to Margaret Rutherford because of the film connection. They also note that Christie casts the film industry as shallow and tasteless in the book.**

From The Mirror Crack'd from Side to Side, Chapter 5

Most people's ideas of Hollywood stars were of sun-bathing by a pool in exotic surroundings and in exotic company. That the climate of Hollywood might be more suited to swimming pools than that of St. Mary Mead failed to be considered. After all, England always has one fine hot week in the summer and there is always one day that the Sunday papers published articles on How to Keep Cool, How to Have Cool Suppers and How to Make Cool Drinks. The pool was almost exactly what everyone had imagined it might be. It was large, its waters were blue, it had a kind of exotic pavilion for changing and was surrounded with a highly artificial plantation of hedges and shrubs. The reactions of the multitude were exactly as might have been expected and hovered over a wide range of remarks.

"O-oh, isn't it lovely?"

"Two penn'orth of splash here, all right!"

"Reminds me of that holiday camp I went to."

"Wicked luxury I call it. It oughtn't to be allowed."

"Look at all that fancy marble. It must have cost the earth!"

"Don't see why these people think they can come over here and spend all the money they like."

Miss Marple on a Horse

MGM produced four Miss Marple films: *Murder She Said* (1961), *Murder at the Gallop* (1963), *Murder Most Foul* (1964), and *Murder Ahoy!* (1964). Each movie diverged further from the plot of the book. Meanwhile, as Agatha later described, her initial resignation to these adaptations shifted to outrage.

Released in June 1963, *Murder at the Gallop*, a loose adaptation of Christie's *After the Funeral* (1953), was an even greater hit with audiences than *Murder She Said*. Like the earlier film, it features Miss Marple in a more active role than in the book. MGM's Miss Marple rides a horse and a bicycle—and even does the twist! Once again, reviewers praised Rutherford. The *Daily Express* said, "The film doesn't need any sets. Close-ups of her face are all that is necessary."

Christie hated the film, as well as *Murder Most Foul* and *Murder Ahoy!*, both of which were released the following year. Finally, in 1964, she wrote a letter to Lawrence P. Bachmann, head of MGM's British division, saying, "I consider you went too far. Miss Marple gallivanting around on horses was ludicrously unlike the original. . . . But worst of all she was never in that book at all. . . . I do not think that you should allow yourself to distort a book you adapt to that extent." Bachmann answered her politely, but as quoted in Richard Hack's Christie biography, he had come to think of her "as an old lady without the first instinct for making film." In making Miss Marple a comedic character, MGM had shifted popular perceptions of the author's mysteries. However grim and cynical, the public now began to think of her fiction even more as quaint. *Cozy*. MGM had effectively solidified the Christie brand.

As the MGM films played in theaters around the world, Christie started writing back-to-back Marple novels. These books were notably dark. *At Bertram's Hotel* is a deeply cynical novel about the value of English rituals and institutions as commodities, for example, and *A Caribbean Mystery* explores the feelings of uselessness and boredom that can come with old age.

THE MORE YOU KNOW

In a letter written on March 18, 1964, to Pat Cork, Edmund Cork's wife, Christie wrote, "I really feel sick and ashamed of what I did when I signed up with MGM. It was my fault. One does things for money and one is wrong to do so—since one parts with one's literary integrity."

Grandmother and Grandson

In 1963, Agatha's grandson, Mathew, turned twenty. Now a student at Oxford studying history, politics, philosophy, and economics, Mathew had a special bond with his grandmother. Agatha had been ecstatic over Mathew's birth on September 21, 1943. "The baby, a large boy," she wrote to Max while he was in the Middle East, "looking so like Hubert to my mind that all he needs is a monocle." While he attended Elstree, a preparatory school, she would drive over from Winterbrook in Max's silver Rolls Royce and take him on picnics, to see Shakespeare at Stratford, or to hear Wagner at Bayreuth. She also sent him each of her stories as soon as they were published.

An imaginative and cheerful child who loved stories, Mathew "resembled Agatha far more than his mother," according to Laura Thompson. He spent part of every summer at Greenway with Rosalind and his stepfather, Anthony Hicks, and he and Agatha would spend hours playing cricket on the lawn, reading, and walking around Greenway's gardens and woods.

Laura Thompson suggests that in Mathew, Agatha could finally release her maternal feelings. The pair were close right up to her death in 1976. He visited her and Max every summer at Greenway, and during the academic year, they would often meet for lunch or attend a play together.

And it was Mathew who approached the painter Oscar Kokoschka to paint a portrait of Agatha in 1969 in anticipation of her eightieth birthday. Though he had primarily retired from portraiture, Kokoschka, also in his eighties and a fan of Christie's fiction, agreed to do so. Artist and sitter did eight two-hour sittings in London, at each of which, according to Janet Morgan, Kokoschka consumed half a bottle of whiskey.

As an adult, Mathew also became heavily involved in Agatha Christie Ltd. In 1969, he established The Agatha Christie Trust for Children, an organization that provides services for children, young people, and people with disabilities. Additionally, it would be Mathew who gifted Greenway, Agatha's beloved home, to the National Trust in 2000, though it remained a private home to Rosalind and Anthony Hicks until after their deaths in 2005.

The More You Know

During the 1960s, Mathew's cousin and Agatha's nephew, James ("Jack") Watts, died at age fifty-seven, having never married. Madge's only child, James, was a student at Oxford and a conservative politician. After his parents died, he sold the family home, Abney Hall, for the low price of about 12,000 pounds, and auctioned off all its furnishings and other belongings. The auction lasted ten days.

From Crooked House, Chapter 26

"Today I killed grandfather."

We turned the pages. It was an amazing production. Interesting, I should imagine, to a psychologist. It set out, with such terrible clarity, the fury of thwarted egoism.

The motive for the crime was set down, pitifully childish and inadequate.

"Grandfather wouldn't let me do bally dancing so I made up my mind I would kill him. Then we would go to London and live and mother wouldn't mind me doing bally."

I give only a few entries. They are all significant.

"I don't want to go to Switzerland—I won't go. If mother makes me I will kill her too—only I can't get any poison. Perhaps I could make it with youberries. They are poisonous, the book says so. Eustace has made me very cross to day. He says I am only a girl and no use and that its silly my detecting. He wouldn't think me silly if he knew it was me did the murder."

The Elder Mallowans

In 1964, while visiting Torquay, Agatha decided to drive to the spot where Ashfield, her beloved childhood home, had once stood. A few years earlier, hearing that the house would soon be demolished to make way for cheap housing, she tried to buy it back. But she was too late. Now, as she would describe, "There was nothing that could even stir a memory. They were the meanest, shoddiest little houses I had ever seen. None of the great trees remained. . . . I could not even determine in my mind where the house had stood."

Scholars argue that this visit, in some ways, set the tone for the remainder of the decade. Agatha's novels, at this point, increasingly explore loss, memory, and decline. She and Max were also both suffering from bouts of ill-health. A smoker and drinker all his life, Max suffered several minor strokes in the 1960s. Agatha, meanwhile, battled bronchitis and gastritis. The couple made their final trip to the Middle East in 1967, Agatha now finding the journey too strenuous. Winterbrook, meanwhile, was slowly falling into decay.

Still, the 1960s and early 1970s also brought joys and rewards for the couple. In 1966, Agatha and Max traveled to America for a two-month stay (they had made an earlier trip in 1956). This time, Agatha told family and friends that she wanted to see the country of her ancestors. But letters from Edmund Cork suggest she had other items on her agenda too: "Be warned," he advised the assistant to Harold Ober, Agatha's American agent. "Agatha told me yesterday that the real object of her visit to America is to pick up some outsize knickers." Two years later, Max was knighted, and Agatha became Lady Mallowan. Then, in 1971, The New Year Honours List announced Agatha's appointment as a Dame Commander of the British Empire (DBE) for her contributions to literature. The investiture ceremony took place at Buckingham Palace, where Agatha was honored by Queen Elizabeth II. Reportedly, the queen said to her, "You've given a great deal of pleasure to a lot of people." Agatha replied, "That's very nice of you to say so, Your Majesty."

Dame Agatha Christie was her last change of name, though friends and acquaintances continued to call her Lady Mallowan. Janet Morgan reports that she did write "DBE" on the line above the title of her notebook for *Nemesis*, her last Marple book.

LITERARY CONNECTIONS

The same year she became a Dame, 1971, Agatha published *Nemesis*. A novel about the sadnesses of love, as well as a detective story, *Nemesis* is described as "Agatha's last masterpiece" by Laura Thompson.

Interviewing Agatha

Agatha Christie hated being interviewed (at a request for a telephone interview, Christie historian Mark Aldridge says, she told her agent's secretary in a typical response to "say I'm too deaf or anything you like"). The sessions she did grant with journalists tended to be superficial in content. Christie fans and scholars can see that what she says in them tends to portray her as indifferent to fame, unconcerned with sales, and haphazard in her approach to writing. "I haven't much method," she said in a BBC interview. Regarding how much money she earned from book sales, she said to another interviewer, "I only know it comes in large blocks and that then there is a dry space."

Christie's most revealing interview was in 1966 with Frances Wyndham, the fiction writer and journalist. Here, she famously referred to herself as "a sausage machine": "Oh, I am an incredible sausage machine. . . . As soon as one is made and cut off the string, I have to think of the next. . . . But probably I could write the same book again and again, and nobody would notice."

Of Poirot, Christie said that he was out of step with current times: "I'm afraid Poirot gets more and more unreal as time goes by. A private detective who takes cases just doesn't exist these days, so it becomes more difficult to involve him.

. . . The problem doesn't arise with Miss Marple: there are still plenty of them drifting about." Christie also explained to Wyndham how she goes about crafting her plots, saying, "You start with the wish to deceive, and then work backwards. I begin with a fairly complete diagram. . . . One's always a *little* self-conscious over the murderer's first appearance. He must never come in too late; that's uninteresting for the reader at the end of the book. And the dénouement has to be worked out frightfully carefully."

Many have wondered why this interview with Wyndham was more revealing and detailed than others. Some propose that perhaps Christie wanted to reassert her professionalism as she grew older and, in the minds of the public, increasingly quaint. Regardless, there would be only one interview she ever agreed to happily: with a schoolboy named David Llewellyn, who knocked on the door of Winterbrook and requested an interview for his school magazine. Impressed by his initiative, Christie later described, she agreed. The interview was published in the *Wallingford Grammar School Magazine* in 1970.

The More You Know

In the Frances Wyndham interview, Agatha observed, "One is very lucky to have writing as a trade. One can work hard at it but also have delicious days of leisure and idleness. Young people nowadays have no time at all for what I call leisure, thinking, and all that."

Adapting Murder on the Orient Express

By 1970, Agatha Christie's agreement with MGM had expired. As Mark Aldridge reports, this termination had the consequence of *other* studios now asking her to bring Poirot to the screen. She said no to each request, gaining a reputation as "Adamant Agatha," as a headline from the *Daily Mirror* called her. The *Mirror* went on to say, "There's a wealth of Agatha Christie material in novels, stories, and plays. Every week her agencies receive inquiries from producers. But Mrs. Christie . . . remains firmly entrenched against both TV and cinema." Mrs. Christie, however, eventually changed her mind.

November 24, 1974, was the world premiere of the film *Murder on the Orient Express*. It was a gala event and among Christie's last public appearances. Now mostly restricted to a wheelchair, she was dressed in mink, her hair done for the occasion, pearls around her neck. She stood up when wheeled over to meet Queen Elizabeth II, who was also attending the premiere. And the film itself impressed and delighted Christie.

The success came about thanks to Lord John Brabourne, a well-known producer of films whom Christie liked. *Murder on the Orient Express* had never been on the screen before. By all accounts, Brabourne was desperate to try it, but he had a tough time convincing Christie's family. Finally, Brabourne and Agatha Christie Ltd. came to an agreement; the company would give him rights to the book under the condition that Poirot would be licensed only for this one appearance.

Brabourne hired Sidney Lumet, the director famous for the film *Twelve Angry Men*. Lumet and Brabourne then got screenwriter Paul Dehn, who had adapted the James Bond novel, *Goldfinger*, to create the script. They also put together a star-studded cast: Lauren Bacall as Mrs. Hubbard, Sean Connery as Lieutenant Colonel Arbuthnot, Ingrid Bergman as Greta Ohlsson, and Albert Finney as Poirot, among others.

The film earned six Academy Award nominations and one win: Ingrid Bergman for Best Supporting Actress. As scholars agree, its artistry and critical reception helped elevate Christie's reputation at a time when critical opinion of her writing had declared it outmoded. The one aspect of the film Christie didn't like was Albert Finney's bombastic performance as Poirot. Most critics didn't like it either. As you'll explore later, it would take another fifteen years before an actor finally seemed to capture Poirot.

THE MORE YOU KNOW

Twelve Angry Men **is a 1957 film starring Henry Fonda. Its storyline shares some key parallels with** ***Murder on the Orient Express*****. Both stories are concerned with the execution of justice by "ordinary" figures outside the law, and both take place within one single closed space.**

Last Gasps

During the last several years of her life, as Christie battled arthritis, physical frailty, and the aftereffects of a heart attack in 1974, she continued writing. Sometime in early 1971, she laid out plans for *Nemesis,* her last Miss Marple novel, and wrote it quickly. It remains one of her most critically acclaimed novels, less a detective story than a somber meditation on love's painful nature.

But there were also less successful moments during these final years. That same year, 1971, Christie tried the theater one last time with "a weak little play," as Laura Thompson describes it. Called *Fiddlers Five,* the play opened in Bristol to a very poor reception. Following this, Rosalind suggested the play not go to London. Agatha snidely wrote to her daughter: "I can't see why you are so opposed to its being a commercial success on tour—if it does turn out to be so—I don't suppose you or Mathew or the Harrison Homes and the rest of those who benefit in the company will really refuse their cut of the takings."

A few months later, in June 1971, Agatha was rushed to Nuffield Hospital in Oxford after breaking her hip in a fall. "Things were critical for a day or two," Max wrote to her agent in America, "but I am delighted to tell you that she has made a miraculous recovery." By the end of the year, Agatha was walking—and writing—again. She traveled to London to be measured for a wax figure at Madame Tussauds waxwork museum, and she began *Elephants Can Remember*, her last Ariadne Oliver book. As she had always done, she delivered this book to Collins on time. It was published at the end of 1972.

That same year, Agatha told Mrs. Thompson, who helped look after things at Greenway, "I'm so tired, and they're waiting for every word I write." "They" were her publishers at Collins. When Rosalind learned this, as Janet Morgan explains, she told Billy Collins not to press for any more books. He agreed to back off—and yet, Christie kept writing. Like Hercule Poirot, Christie worked until the very end of her life.

LITERARY CONNECTIONS

The Christie works that appeared between 1971 and 1976 are *The Golden Ball and Other Stories* (1971); *Nemesis* (1971); *Elephants Can Remember* (1972); *Fiddlers Three* (1972), a play (reworked from *Fiddlers Five*); *Poems* (1973); *Postern of Fate* (1973); *Poirot's Early Cases* (1974); *Curtain* (1975); and *Sleeping Murder* (1976).

Curtains for Poirot

Curtain and *Sleeping Murder*, the two novels in which Christie's popular detectives, Poirot and Marple, respectively, solve their final cases, had been sitting in the London office of Collins for over three decades. Christie had written them during the war, as "insurance" against her possible untimely death. It had been the plan to release them posthumously.

But in 1975, as Christie's health deteriorated, it was agreed that *Curtain* should be published. Appearing in September of that year, the novel depicts Poirot as dying and shrunken. Hastings, his old friend and sidekick, returns to England to find him "crippled with arthritis. . . . His once plump frame had fallen in." *Curtain* portrays Poirot's last case as a serial killing. Here, the perpetrator arranges situations where otherwise respectable, law-abiding people wind up killing, or wishing to kill, others. Recalling Sir Arthur Conan Doyle's villain, Moriarty, the killer does no killing himself; rather, he works his evil into others. In the end, Poirot puts a stop to his crimes.

The upcoming publication of *Curtain* prompted *The New York Times* to do something it had never done before and has never done since. On August 6, 1975, readers opened the paper to find an obituary not of an actual person but of a character:

Poirot. The obituary began: "Hercule Poirot, a Belgian detective who became internationally famous, is dead. His age is unknown." The *Times* piece also reflected on Christie's own career: "Her hold on her audience is remarkable in a way because the kind of fiction she writes is, well, not exactly contemporary. Her characters come from the quiet and exceedingly comfortable middle class. . . . The houses in her fiction are spacious, teas are frequent and abundant, servants abound."

Referencing the "comfortable" aspects of Christie's fiction, the critic not only called her work out of step with contemporary life but, like others before him, also portrayed her as a *cozy* mystery writer, ignoring the dark elements of her works. In the decades ahead, many TV and film adaptations of Christie's novels would do the same, playing up her use of quaint villages, the eccentricity of some of her characters, and the comedic touch often found in her dialogue. Of course, earlier films like the MGM Marple movies, the 1965 detective comedy *The Alphabet Murders,* and even Billy Wilder's *Witness for the Prosecution* had all done the same.

LITERARY CONNECTIONS

Many critics praised *Curtain* for its "skillful solution," emotional weight, and morally ambiguous ending. Francis Wyndham, writing for *The Times Literary Supplement,* remarked, "As she presumably intended, in this one Agatha Christie has brought off the bluff to end them all."

From Curtain, Chapter 13

"By taking Norton's life, I have saved other lives—innocent lives. But still I do not know. . . . It is perhaps right that I should not know. I have always been so sure—too sure . . .

But now I am very humble and I say like a little child: 'I do not know . . .'

Good-bye, *cher ami*. I have moved the amyl nitrite ampoules away from beside my bed. I prefer to leave myself in the hands of the *bon Dieu*. May his punishment, or his mercy, be swift!

We shall not hunt together again, my friend. Our first hunt was here—and our last . . .

They were good days.

Yes, they have been good days . . ."

End of Hercule Poirot's manuscript.

Appointment with Death

In 1974, Agatha had a heart attack, and her doctor prescribed a medicine that caused her to lose more than half her weight. She ate and drank very little but remained a good sport, "tottering to Wimbledon with Max," as Janet Morgan details. In June, Antony Armstrong-Jones, 1st Earl of Snowdon, came to Winterbrook to interview and photograph Agatha. As he described later, he found a frail, shrunken woman. When he asked Agatha how she'd like to be remembered, she replied, "as a rather good writer of detective stories."

She and Max were spending all their time at Winterbrook now. After turning eighty, it was clear she was and felt old, as Janet Morgan describes. But in 1973, she wrote *Postern of Fate*. She struggled to concentrate throughout and needed the assistance of Max, as well as of Daphne Honeybone, who typed for both Mallowans, to tidy up the manuscript after she wrote it. The novel is remarkable for how much of it is filled with autobiographical bits about Agatha's childhood. One notebook, written in by Agatha later that year, shows plans for developing another novel: "A cookery story. About: a meringue?" The book never got written.

Sometime in the summer of 1975, Agatha started to sleep downstairs, no longer able to climb the stairs to hers and Max's bedroom. In December, she fell through the

French doors at Winterbrook and badly split her head. But she mustered enough strength to visit the voting polls to vote yes for England's membership in the European Community and to argue with Collins about a jacket cover for *Poirot's Early Cases* that made Poirot look tall.

And then, on January 12, 1976, Agatha died of "natural causes." Max said, "As I wheeled her out in her chair after luncheon to the drawing-room . . . death came as a merciful release, though it has left me with a feeling of emptiness after forty-five years of a loving and merry companionship." In London, the audience attending *The Mousetrap* at the time of her death stood in silent tribute. The Savoy and St. Martins Lanes hotels, places where she had been feted and celebrated, dimmed their lights. She was buried with her wedding ring at St. Mary's Church, Cholsey. Several months later, in May, there was a memorial service at St. Martin-in the-Fields, with her publisher, Billy Collins, delivering an address.

The More You Know

Recently, it has been suggested that Agatha was probably suffering from Alzheimer's disease toward the end of her life. In 2009, Ian Lancashire and Graeme Hirst of the University of Toronto did an extensive digital study of her works that shows a dramatic decrease in vocabulary as she aged: one symptom of the disease. Since then, those who knew her have said she often got angry and complained of an inability to concentrate, two additional symptoms of Alzheimer's.

After Agatha

Following Agatha's death, there was the question of what would happen to her estate. One issue was Greenway, her beloved Georgian home. The problems with owning such a large estate had increasingly fallen on Rosalind and her second husband, Anthony, since the early 1950s. Agatha and Max were still traveling to Iraq during that decade, so Rosalind assumed charge of the house and gardens. To avoid tax, Agatha sold Greenway to Rosalind in 1959, and in 1967, Rosalind and Anthony moved in. The couple stayed there until Rosalind's death in 2004 at age eighty-five.

Another issue was Agatha Christie Ltd. At the time of Agatha's death, it had already been divided up. In 1968, 51 percent of the company had been sold to Booker-McConnell (the company that established the Booker Prize in 1969) to pay off Agatha's enormous tax debts. By 1972, Booker had also acquired the interest on copyrights owned by the Christie Copyrights Trust. The company had lent Agatha the money she needed to pay off the British revenue service, securing their loan with the copyrights still in her possession. In her eighties, Agatha thus owed a personal debt to Booker (paid with the money left in her estate), but was finally free of the revenue service, which had troubled her for over thirty years.

There was also the question of how she and her novels would be remembered. By all accounts, Rosalind took charge of that; in fact, she had been doing so since the 1950s. She scoured the press for negative reviews of her mother's books or insulting comments about Agatha, refused one request after another by authors wishing to write a Christie biography until she finally granted Janet Morgan permission for an authorized one (it came out in 1984), shut down any mention of the events of 1926, and railed at adaptations she found unfaithful to the novels.

"After her mother's death she became as fierce as a lioness in Agatha's defense," says Laura Thompson. Some biographers speculate that Rosalind felt guilty for her past behavior, and this protectiveness of her mother's legacy was a means of mitigating that guilt. Others suggest that safeguarding Agatha's estate, which she did until she died, finally gave Rosalind a life purpose.

THE MORE YOU KNOW

Agatha's will purportedly left a total of 106,683 pounds (about 723,000 pounds today). As biographers note, it was an astonishingly small sum given the money her books had made over six prolific decades.

Mrs. Mallowan #2

After Agatha's death, Max continued to live at Winterbrook, "Max's house," as Agatha had called it. On friendly terms with Rosalind, Max saw her and her family regularly. He still had friends from the days of his archaeological digs who came to visit him as well—one in particular. That friend was Barbara Hastings Parker, an archaeologist who had been his assistant at Nimrud and the secretary and librarian of the British School of Archaeology (BSA) in Iraq. She had been with him on the day of Agatha's death.

Roughly eighteen months later, in September 1977, Max married Barbara in a quiet ceremony. He had written Rosalind a few months before, informing her of his plans to marry Barbara, knowing that his stepdaughter didn't much care for her (as one interviewee of Thompson's claims, Rosalind found Barbara annoying and was "very possessive, very very possessive of her [Agatha's] memory"). "No one will ever take the place of my dear Agatha," Max wrote Rosalind, "but I think she would have approved. . . . It is lonely now, and will not be so with Barbara who has always been a devoted friend."

Thin with large eyes, Barbara had been a model. She had also studied Chinese at the Courtauld, an independent college of the University of London specializing in art history, curation, and preservation. In 1940, she was invited to run the BSA house in Baghdad where Max and Agatha regularly took up a monthly residence before heading out to Max's excavation sites. Soon, Barbara was helping Max with a variety of tasks.

By all accounts, Barbara's real contribution to Max's work lay in her ability to navigate Iraqi society. Fluent in Arabic, it was she who made the necessary connections to ensure the success of Max's excavations. Some think that Max and Barbara had a long-term affair dating as far back as the 1940s or 1950s while he and Agatha were married; others insist not.

Max and Barbara lived together for barely a year at Winterbrook. Then, on August 19, 1978, Max Mallowan died of acute myocardial failure (a medical emergency where blood flow to a part of the heart is blocked)—and was buried alongside his first wife at St. Mary's Church.

LITERARY CONNECTIONS

By all accounts, Barbara Hastings Parker was the physical model for Valerie Hobhouse in the Poirot novel *Hickory Dickory Dock* (1955). A beauty salon owner involved in a smuggling racket, Valerie is described by her landlady as "a clever dark girl with rather a sarcastic way of talking." Later in the novel, when readers first see her, Valerie is "prone on a sofa, with her elegant feet stuck up over the arm of it." She talks "with a lazy drawling voice."

Miss Marple on the Small Screen

It was Boxing Day in the UK, 1984. Christie had been dead for eight years, a beloved author still missed by millions. That night, the BBC launched a new TV series, *Miss Marple*, with its adaptation of *The Body in the Library*. The show was an immediate hit in the UK, as well as in America, where it aired on PBS's *Mystery!*

Christie hated almost every adaptation she'd seen of her work. She also "did not much care for television," according to Max Mallowan. But many believe Christie would have loved the BBC's *Miss Marple*. Faithful to the original work, the series starred Joan Hickson, the actress to whom, nearly forty years earlier, Christie had written, "I hope one day you will play my dear Miss Marple." Aware of how resistant Christie was to having her works adapted, producer Pat Sandys of London Weekend Television had first approached Mathew Prichard and the Christie estate with a researched, detailed plan to film the non-Marple novels *Why Didn't They Ask Evans?* and *The Seven Dials Mystery* in the early 1980s. Both adaptations did so well that Prichard then gave BBC the rights to all twelve Marple novels.

Running from 1984 to 1992, the series featured twelve episodes. In addition to Miss Marple, Christie's detectives

Inspector Slack and Detective Sergeant Lake regularly appeared on the show, along with other familiars like Dolly Bantry and Miss Marple's nephew, Raymond West. The tone of the show is light and nostalgic. All the episodes take place in the 1950s, most of them set in quaint villages (Nether Wollop in Hampshire served as St. Mary Mead) and rural landscapes.

At the time she began playing Miss Marple, Joan Hickson was seventy-eight years old (the oldest performer ever to take the lead in a TV series). A character actress with a background in comedy, she had made a career on stage, film, and television playing maids and batty old ladies, just like Margaret Rutherford. "I was never the star because I don't think I've ever been a great actress," Hickson once said. "I've never done anything except get on with my work. In some ways, I'm probably just like another Miss Marple." Joan Hickson died in October 1998 at age ninety-two. She is buried in Devon, the land of Agatha Christie.

THE MORE YOU KNOW

Joan Hickson's connection to Christie goes well beyond the TV series. She also did audiobooks of Miss Marple novels; played a minor role in the 1937 film *Love from a Stranger*, an adaptation of Christie's play of the same name; and played the housekeeper in *Murder She Said* (1961), one of the MGM adaptations that Agatha hated.

Agatha Christie's Poirot

Amid the success of the BBC's *Miss Marple*, competitors tried their hand at adapting Agatha Christie. And on January 8, 1989, ITV launched *Agatha Christie's Poirot*. It would air for twenty-five years, making it the longest-running series on PBS's *Mystery!* With seventy episodes spanning thirteen seasons, the show had adapted every major work featuring Poirot by the time it ended on November 13, 2013.

For its first eight seasons, *Agatha Christie's Poirot* followed the convention of Golden Age mysteries, portraying a world where threats to social stability seem easily identifiable and foiled. David Suchet, the actor who played Poirot, described the setting as "a world where manners and morals are quite different from today. . . . He [Poirot] lives in a simpler, some would say more human, era."

With the biggest budget of a crime drama to date, the series included lush interior sets, gorgeous clothes, on-location shooting, and characters enjoying expensive vacations. Poirot's set designers also took special care with the detective's two apartments. They purchased English designer pottery and art deco figures, placed silk and velvet accents everywhere, filled porcelain vases with flowers, and made sure to use furniture with square shapes because Poirot hates curves.

Another reason for the show's success was Poirot's three sidekicks: Captain Arthur Hastings, Miss Lemon, and Inspector Japp. "I do think, for a television series, you need a basic family unit, whether it's a family or not," said Clive Exton, the creator and principal screenwriter for the series. These three characters were Poirot's family until 2004 when they disappeared from the series, as had Exton.

The shift started in 2002, when Granada took over production of the series from London Weekend Television. They made it clear they wanted the show to have a darker tone. The series still had moments of comedy and affection, mainly in the scenes where Poirot interacts with Ariadne Oliver or his butler, George. But it now featured motifs like abortion and drug abuse, and Poirot was depicted as increasingly alienated from the world around him. Some viewers disliked the changes, but others saw them as a means of making Poirot a more complex figure who reflected on the cruelties and horrors he had witnessed in his profession and who was coming to terms with his own mortality.

The More You Know

When Granada took over *Agatha Christie's Poirot,* it expanded each episode to the film length of two hours. It also brought in actors who would go on to achieve great fame, including Toby Jones, Jessica Chastain, Barbara Hershey, Benedict Cumberbatch, Emily Blunt, Damian Lewis, and Lesley Manville.

Becoming Poirot

By almost everyone's estimation, including that of Queen Elizabeth II and Agatha Christie's daughter, Rosalind, David Suchet is the definitive Poirot, eclipsing such Poirots as Charles Laughton, Albert Finney, John Malkovich, and Kenneth Branagh.

A method actor who claims to be a fusspot himself, Suchet studied Poirot carefully. He read all the novels and stories featuring Poirot, taking detailed notes and assembling a "dossier" of "Poirotian traits" that he carried in his pocket whenever on set. "It was my business not only to know what he was like, but to gradually become him," Suchet said. By the time he finished composing his file, he knew that Poirot took five lumps of sugar in his tea, three in his coffee; that he waxed his mustache daily; and that he always wore striped pants on his visits to the bank.

During filming in Season 1, Suchet insisted that before Poirot sat down on a public bench, he would place a handkerchief there first. The director, Edward Bennett, reportedly thought the notion ridiculous. But Suchet refused to shoot the scene until Bennett agreed. It was also Suchet who invented Poirot's distinct walk. Christie has described Poirot as having a "rapid, mincing gait." The description confused

Suchet for weeks—until he remembered actor Laurence Olivier's account of how he learned to walk like a Restoration fop: "I put a penny between the cheeks of my bum, old boy, and tried my best to keep it there."

Despite these comic touches, Suchet aimed (and many believe succeeded) to transform his character into a figure of compassion, pride, loneliness, and implacable principles. "He was as real to me as he had been to her [Christie]," Suchet said in his memoir. And thanks to screenwriters like Clive Exton and Anthony Horowitz, Suchet's Poirot is portrayed as a romantic figure easily touched by beauty, as well as a lonely man hampered by his own comic appearance and compulsions. Suchet's Poirot desires romantic love, which always eludes him.

In 2011, David Suchet was appointed Commander of the Order of the British Empire (CBE). He was knighted in 2020 for services to drama.

LITERARY CONNECTIONS

In 2013, David Suchet published a memoir, *Poirot and Me*, about his role as Hercule Poirot. In the acknowledgments, he thanks "the late Rosalind Hicks, Dame Agatha's daughter, and the late Anthony Hicks, who believed that I was capable of bringing Poirot to life for an audience around the world, a view that was reinforced by their son Mathew Prichard. I could not have created and sustained Poirot without their help."

Agatha Christie's Marple

With *Agatha Christie's Poirot* doing so well, ITV decided it was time for a new Miss Marple series. Nearly twenty years had gone by since the BBC had launched its version of the beloved old-lady detective. ITV's show, the producers determined, would be more polished and tongue-in-cheek. And so *Agatha Christie's Marple*, or *Marple*, launched in the UK during the Christmas season, 2004. The show ran for six seasons, producing twenty-three episodes by the time it ended in 2013. Geraldine McEwan played Miss Marple from 2004 to 2009, Julia McKenzie from 2009 to 2013. Following the sixth season, the BBC once again acquired the rights to the Marple stories and novels—ending the ITV series.

Marple departs a lot from the original stories. The series' screenwriters changed the endings, introduced new characters, switched roles, and sometimes altered the identity of the killer. In "The Murder at the Vicarage," they gave Miss Marple a backstory in which she's in love with a married man.

Marple also exaggerates Marple's old-lady traits, costuming McEwan in dresses that look like doilies and McKenzie in sturdy tweed suits; heightens the sinister plots; and pokes fun at Christie conventions like Marple's penchant for gardening. Each episode also pairs Miss Marple with a handsome young inspector or amateur sleuth, played by actors like Matthew MacFayden, Benedict Cumberbatch, John Hannah, Hugh Bonneville, Laurence Fox, and Tom Hughes. Critics agree that visually, the show is gorgeous, with lots of manor homes, spectacular British scenery, and elegant period detail.

McEwan and McKenzie had very different takes on the Marple role. With a long background in comedy, McEwan said she played Marple "as lighter and flightier [than Joan Hickson] with a twinkle . . ." McEwan retired from the role in 2009 because she had fallen and broken her hip. Like Agatha, Julia McKenzie had once trained to be an opera singer. She went on to star in musicals throughout the 1960s and 1970s. In the 1980s, she made her name as a television comedy star. Her Marple, however, is regarded as both more serious and more sensible than McEwan's. McKenzie said: "It's difficult because Agatha Christie wrote her in two ways. . . . First, very much what Geraldine McEwan played: a slight, rather Victorian creature. Then, a little sturdier and tweedier. I chose the latter."

LITERARY CONNECTIONS

ITV's *Marple* adapted all twelve of the Marple novels. In addition, several short stories featuring Miss Marple were adapted for the series. These include "The Blue Geranium" and "Greenshaw's Folly." Several novels in which Miss Marple is not featured—including *The Secret of Chimneys* (1925), *Why Didn't They Ask Evans?* (1934), and *Endless Night* (1967)—were reworked to include her.

From Nemesis, Chapter 5

"Murders as reported in the press have never claimed my attention. I have never read books on criminology as a subject or really been interested in such a thing. No, it has just happened that I have found myself in the vicinity of murder rather more often than would seem normal."

The Case of the "Architecturally Implausible" Mustache

In early November 2017, a new adaptation of *Murder on the Orient Express* opened in theaters worldwide. Previews promised lots of action, a glamorous train setting, and a sterling cast that included Judi Dench, Johnny Depp, Penélope Cruz, and Kenneth Branagh, who also directed the film.

Orient starts off with shots of a boy running back and forth to find two perfectly shaped eggs for a mysterious man whose back is turned to viewers. Then, the camera cuts to a close-up of Branagh's face as Poirot—and his distinct mustache. One reviewer called it "architecturally implausible." Others, "ridiculous," "absurd," "an imbecilic affectation." Some mention of it can be found in every review of the film, evidence for critics of Branagh's "tendency toward excess."

Yet critics also found much to applaud in *Orient* and the two other Christie adaptations that followed it, also directed by Branagh: *Death on the Nile* (2022) and *A Haunting in Venice* (2023), the latter a reworking of Christie's *Hallowe'en Party*, published in 1969. They praised the films for their opulent styling, performances, humor, and the ways they invest Christie's dialogue-heavy novels with action. *Orient* was a box-office success, as was *Death on the Nile*; and while

Haunting didn't fare as well in theaters, its ratings were high on streaming platforms.

Branagh set out to rework Christie's stories through several key strategies. One strategy was to play up the exotic locales where the novels are set while capturing Christie's fascination with travel. Characters in the Branagh adaptations are *on the move,* shuttling across landscapes, hopping on boats, boarding trains. He also diversified the cast, including Black and Asian characters as well as gay characters.

He aimed to turn what could be limitations from a director's point of view into powerful effect. For example, the plot of *Murder on the Orient Express,* formally structured around twelve interviews, becomes a way of exploiting each actor's particular skills. These skills include Michelle Pfeiffer's gift for comedy and Judi Dench's ability to "feel and be in the moment," as Branagh once described.

In 2024, 20th Century Studios announced that they were open to doing more movies based on Christie's works, naming Miss Marple, *And Then There Were None,* and *Witness for the Prosecution* as possibilities.

LITERARY CONNECTIONS

Kenneth Branagh has expressed interest in adapting *The Murder of Roger Ackroyd,* one of his favorite Christie novels. Rights to the novel became public in 2021.

Sarah Phelps and the Christie Quintet

Screenwriter Sarah Phelps had never read any Christie fiction when she was approached about an adaptation. What she'd seen and heard of it—"cosy Sunday night fare," as she called it in a Substack interview—had turned her off: "I thought I knew who she [Christie] was and what her books were. I was an idiot." Then, in 2014, the BBC planned to release an adaptation of Christie's bestselling novel, *And Then There Were None,* to celebrate the 125th anniversary of her birthday. Wanting something darker than previous TV adaptations, they turned to Sarah Phelps. Known for her work on *EastEnders,* a soap opera–style series tackling taboo subjects, Phelps had a history of adapting classic novels (*Oliver Twist* in 2007 and *Great Expectations* in 2011) into moody, bleak stories expunged of their original humor. Phelps read Christie's novel and was blown away by how "remorselessly cruel it was." She accepted the BBC's offer to adapt it.

As Phelps began working on the script, Britain conducted the EU referendum, in which the country voted to leave the European Union. This historical event inspired her to pitch an idea to the BBC: Rather than adapt one novel by Christie, why not five? Her vision was to show the changes in Britain between the end of World War I and the 1960s through Christie's novels. Her focus would be a new twist on Christie's question of who the murderer was: "*What* killed the victim? Not just the murder weapon but *what* condition, *what* atmosphere, *what* dynamic, both domestic and national, created the volatile dangerous environment where a person has their life ripped from them? So, anyway, I pitched it and . . . it happened." Phelps was also inspired, she says, by the remorselessness of Greek tragedy.

The resulting shows in the quintet were *And Then There Were None* (2015), *Witness for the Prosecution* (2016), *The ABC Murders* (2018), *Ordeal by Innocence* (2018), and *The Pale Horse* (2020). Each show is either a two- or three-part miniseries produced with large budgets, lush sets, on-location filming, and high-profile casts. Actors in the series include Emily Blunt, Charles Dance, Bill Nighy, and John Malkovich. Viewer response to the quintet has been mixed. Some disapproved of the radical changes made to the stories. Others praised these darker spins on the novels.

THE MORE YOU KNOW

A critic for *The Guardian* wrote of Sarah Phelps's work: "The latest adaptations, rich, dark, adult, and drawing on a backdrop of postwar grief and instability, are a far cry from the sunny—still murderous, but sunny—uplands [of Joan Hickson's Miss Marple] or the light-filled art deco apartments in which the *leetle* grey cells of David Suchet's Poirot could do their work. The audience's innocence has been too battered by the ordeals of the past few years, perhaps, for them to pass muster now."

New Literary Imaginings

While film and television continue to develop new takes on Agatha Christie, recent novelists have been revisiting her life and work in historical fiction. The most acclaimed of these books offer a complex psychological portrait of the author while exploring such central themes in her work as betrayal, respectability as camouflage, and the social disruptions caused by war.

One such novel is Marie Benedict's *The Mystery of Mrs. Christie* (2020), which speculates on what could have happened during Christie's eleven-day disappearance. A *New York Times* bestselling author who's written about the lives of women like Clementine Churchill and Mileva Einstein, Benedict tells the story of Christie's courtship, marriage, and disappearance from two perspectives: Agatha's and Archie's. Critics praised the novel for its ingenious plot twists, double narration, and psychological exploration of both Christies.

Another historical novel that has garnered high praise is *The Christie Affair* (2022) by Nina de Gramont. Imagining Agatha's disappearance from the point of view of Archie Christie's mistress, Nancy Neele (called Miss Nan O'Dea in the novel), de Gramont offers an intricate character study of the two women. With feminist intent, she portrays Christie as the "architect of her own disappearance."

A Talent for Murder (2017) by Andrew Wilson also numbers among the most acclaimed historical novels about Christie. A biographer of Patricia Highsmith and Sylvia Plath, among others, Wilson creates a plot with multiple twists. In the novel, Christie meets a doctor, an "utter sadist," who inveigles her in a plot involving murder and blackmail. "I am convinced that, had you not had the outlet of your books . . . you yourself may even have been tempted to commit a heinous crime," he tells her. The novel also has shifting points of view, recalling writers like Virginia Woolf and Patricia Highsmith. Wilson portrays Christie as psychologically damaged, tormented by painful memories and murderous thoughts. He draws on such biographical elements as her father's early death and her experiences as a wartime nurse, as well as her husband's infidelity.

LITERARY CONNECTIONS

Other novels that offer a twist on Christie's life include *Murder at Mallowan Hall* (2021) by Colleen Cambridge, which follows Phyllida Bright, a fictional housekeeper (and amateur sleuth) who works for Christie and Max Mallowan. Also of note is *The Agathas* (2022) by Kathleen Glasgow and Liz Lawson, following teenage detectives who are Christie fans.

Correcting Christie

In 2023, HarperCollins announced that it would be "re-editing" Christie's novels to eliminate all instances of potentially offensive language, including racial and ethnic insults and stereotyping. Earlier, it had performed similar re-edits on writers Roald Dahl and Ian Fleming. As HarperCollins explained of these changes, "The updates follow edits made to books by Roald Dahl and Ian Fleming to remove offensive references to gender and race in a bid to preserve their relevance to modern readers. . . . The edits cut references to ethnicity, such as describing a character as black, Jewish, or Gypsy, or a female character's torso as 'of black marble' and a judge's 'Indian temper,' and removed terms such as 'Oriental' and the N-word. The word 'natives' has been replaced with the word 'locals.'" In some cases, the edits involved removal of a word; in other cases, removal of entire passages. The result has been a new edition of novels for Christie (and Dahl and Fleming).

The decision to edit these writers has sparked controversy, especially in Christie's case. Accusations of censorship have come from free speech groups and from PEN America, the writers' organization. Some complain that in editing Christie, readers lose the sense of an author writing in a particular time and place. Others point out that the cuts to the speech or thoughts of Christie's characters flatten their portrayal while leaving viewers with less-developed situations.

One passage from Christie's *Death on the Nile* has become a linchpin in the controversy. In the original novel, the character of Mrs. Allerton, a provincial middle-aged woman who grows more compassionate as the novel progresses, complains early on that a group of local children are pestering her. She says, "They come back and stare, and stare, and their eyes are simply disgusting, and so are their noses, and I don't believe I really like children." The passage has been stripped down in a new edition to state, "They come back and stare, and stare. And I don't believe I really like children." Those engaged in the debate point to the *Nile* passage as an example of how complex the process of "re-editing" can be.

LITERARY CONNECTIONS

Many of the recent Christie film and TV adaptations have eliminated, or endeavored to correct, the offensive elements of the author's work. One strategy has been to cast actors of color in some of the principal roles, such as Georgina Campbell as Delphine Easterbrook in *The Pale Horse* (2020) or Crystal Clarke as Tina Argyll in *Ordeal by Innocence* (2018). In the recent TV adaptation of *Murder Is Easy* (2023), Christie's white protagonist, Luke Fitzwilliam, becomes a Nigerian attaché played by Black actor David Jonsson. *Seven Dials* (2026) cast Nabhaan Rizwan, of Indian descent, as the character of Ronnie Devereux and *Agatha Christie's Tommy & Tuppence* (2026) cast Black actress Antonia Thomas as Tuppence.

Christie Unbound

Agatha Christie's works continue to inspire new projects in film, television, drama, and literature. Among the upcoming adaptations is a new Miss Marple TV series produced by James Prichard. Agatha's great-grandson and CEO of Agatha Christie Ltd., Prichard feels that "Poirot has stolen [Marple's] limelight for a very long time." He sees Miss Marple as an "underestimated" character and hopes to produce a "lighter" adaptation that will reinvent the iconic detective for modern tastes and sensibilities.

Kenneth Branagh has also hinted that he hopes to adapt *The Murder of Roger Ackroyd.* This would be the fourth film adaptation of a Christie novel he has undertaken. Meanwhile, a Netflix version of *The Seven Dials Mystery,* set for release on Netflix on Jan. 15, 2026, is underway. Scripted by *Broadchurch* creator Chris Chibnall, the adaptation will appear as a three-part series. Its cast includes Helena Bonham Carter and Martin Freeman. As with many Christie novels, *Seven Dials* features a feisty young woman (Mia McKenna-Bruce) who blossoms into an amateur sleuth.

While *Seven Dials,* published in 1929, is one of Christie's early novels, *Endless Night,* which the BBC has announced it is adapting, is among her last. Originally released in October

1967, *Endless Night* focuses on a murderous young charmer named Michael Rogers who concocts a plan to seduce, marry, and murder a wealthy young woman. *Endless Night* is a thriller, viewed by fans as darker and more psychologically complex than most of Christie's other novels. The BBC plans to make it a three-part series, scripted by Sarah Phelps. It will be Phelps's sixth Agatha Christie adaptation.

HarperCollins also plans to release a new Miss Marple novel written by bestselling thriller author Lucy Foley. Having sold over 5 million copies worldwide, Foley's books are often compared to Christie's. *The Guardian*, in fact, calls her an "Agatha Christie for the Instagram Age." Of Miss Marple, Foley says she loves "the way she uses her invisibility . . . as her superpower." Due to be released on September 8, 2026, Foley's novel, *Murder at the Grand Alpine Hotel*, capitalizes on Christie's penchant for luxurious, remote settings as crime scenes while putting Miss Marple right at the center of a murder investigation.

LITERARY CONNECTIONS

Lucy Foley's novels include *The Book of Lost and Found* (2015), *The Invitation* (2016), *Last Letter from Istanbul* (2018), *The Hunting Party* (2019), *The Guest List* (2020), *The Paris Apartment* (2022), and *The Midnight Feast* (2024). Similar to Christie's works, Foley's stories are often set in isolated locales with a limited group of potential victims and suspects.

Further Reading

- *Agatha Christie: An Autobiography*. By Agatha Christie. William Morrow—Written between 1950 and 1965, Christie's lively narrative highlights the happier moments of her life, especially her childhood.
- *Agatha Christie: A Biography*. By Janet Morgan. Alfred A. Knopf—The first authorized biography of Christie, written with the use of her private papers and family contributions.
- *Agatha Christie: An Elusive Woman*. By Lucy Worsley. Pegasus Crime—This book seeks to rescue Christie from popular misperceptions of her life and work by stressing their darker, more modern elements.
- *Agatha Christie: A Mysterious Life*. By Laura Thompson. Pegasus Crime—This biography seeks to go inside Christie's mind, relying heavily on her fiction to explain her thoughts and emotions.
- *Agatha Christie: The Woman and Her Mysteries*. By Gillian Gill. The Free Press—Published in 1990, this biography stresses the feminist elements of Christie's fiction and life decisions.
- *Agatha Christie's Marple: Expert on Wickedness*. By Mark Aldridge. HarperCollins—Similar to *Agatha Christie's Poirot*, this book is a compendium of interesting facts about the Miss Marple novels and stories and the theatrical, television, and cinematic adaptations they inspired.

- *Agatha Christie's Poirot: The Greatest Detective in the World*. By Mark Aldridge. HarperCollins—A compendium of Poirot that explores Christie's fiction and the legacy of theatrical, film, and television adaptations featuring the Belgian detective.
- *Agatha Christie's Secret Notebooks: Fifty Years of Mystery in the Making*. By John Curran. Harper—A collection of Christie's private notebooks, with pages reproduced to show how Christie plotted and devised ideas for her novels.
- *The Bloomsbury Handbook to Agatha Christie*. By Mary Anna Evans and J.C. Bernthal, editors. Bloomsbury Academic—A collection of twenty essays and an introduction, most of them scholarly, that cover topics such as feminism, queerness, World Wars I and II, and race.
- *Curtain Up: Agatha Christie: A Life in the Theatre*. By Julius Green. Harper—The seminal book on Christie's career in theater.
- *The Grand Tour: Around the World with the Queen of Mystery*. By Mathew Prichard, editor. HarperCollins—A coffee-table-style book brimming with photos of Agatha's 1922 trip around the world and excerpts of letters she wrote back home.
- *The Life and Crimes of Agatha Christie: A Biographical Companion to the Works of Agatha Christie*. By Charles Osborne. HarperCollins—A lively, comprehensive guide to Christie's fiction in chronological order, covering her fiction, poetry, and theatrical writing. Chapters include excerpts from reviews, anecdotes, and plot summaries.

Index